SUPERFOODS

RECIPES&PREPARATION

The information in this book should not be treated as a substitute for professional medical advice. Neither the author nor the publisher can be held responsible for any claim or damage arising out of the use, or misuse, of the information in this book.

Saskia Fraser is a healthy-foods expert, author and lifestyle coach. She has helped thousands of busy working women to experience greater energy, mental clarity and self-confidence. Saskia runs online raw-food detoxes and coaching workshops, as well as one-to-one life-coaching programmes. She is the author of *Raw Freedom*, a raw-food recipe book for busy lives, as well as a popular healthy-living blog and two other books for Flame Tree: *Raw Food* and *Vegan Food*. Find her at saskiafraser.com

Publisher & Creative Director: Nick Wells
Senior Project Editor: Catherine Taylor
Copy Editor: Kathy Steer
Art Director: Mike Spender
Layout Design: Jane Ashley
Digital Design & Production: Chris Herbert
Proofreader: Dawn Laker

Special thanks to Carolyn Bingley, George Nash, Kelly Auricchio and Frances Bodiam.

FLAME TREE PUBLISHING
6 Melbray Mews, Fulham,
London SW6 3NS, United Kingdom
www.flametreepublishing.com

This edition first published 2018.

Copyright © 2018 Flame Tree Publishing Ltd

18 20 22 21 19
1 3 5 7 9 10 8 6 4 2

ISBN: 978-1-78664-792-4

A copy of the CIP data for this book is available from the British Library.

Printed in China

Picture Credits

© Stockfood and the following: Wischnewski, Jan 39tl, 161, 175, 186; Eising Studio - Food Photo & Video 63, 77, 113, 151 & 224, 152; Gräfe & Unzer Verlag 82; Jalag / Hoersch, Julia 95; kleine Holthaus, Thorsten 110; Streeter, Clive 118, 173; Gräfe & Unzer Verlag / Neubauer, Mathias 125; PhotoCuisine / Velsberg 126; Sporrer, Brigitte 133; Gräfe & Unzer Verlag / Kramp + Gölling 143; Adsbol, Mikkel 147; Joy Skipper FoodStyling 153; Castilho, Rua 167; Tolhurst, Charlotte 168; für ZS Verlag / Walter, Alexander 180; Gräfe & Unzer Verlag / Schütz, Anke 191; Gräfe & Unzer Verlag / Riis, René 197; The Picture Pantry 201. Courtesy of Shutterstock.com and the following: Ivanna Grigorova 1; Subbotina Anna 3; Lukas Gojda 4; Karissaa 6r; vm2002 6l; Maria Medvedeva 7l; Prostock-studio 7r; 9dream studio 9; beats1 13t, 20; Foxys Forest Manufacture 13b, 14tr, 14b, 14tl, 93, 131, front cover; Evgenia Eliseeva 16r; Zheltyshev 16l; Ekaterina Kondratova 17l, 33tl; Shulevskyy Volodymyr 17r, 36bl; Stolyevych Yuliya 19; iMarzi 23t; nafterphoto 23br; PosiNote 23bl; Lifestyle_Studio 24l; OksankaFra 24r; taa22 25r; zannaz 25l; Efired 27tl; JulijaDmitrijeva 27b; mama_mia 27tr, 206; marilyn barbone 28; Anna Ok 29l; PiercarloAbate 29r; Gayane 30bl; morisfoto 30br; rangizzz 30t; Larisa Blinova 33b, 185; sebra 33tr; sarsmis 35, 163 & back cover top right; KAppleyard 36t; mongione 36br; Anna_Pustynnikova 39tr, 48tl, 216 ; Brent Hofacker 39br, 117, 141; Odua Images 39bl; Magdanatka 40t; Sentelia 40br; ULKASTUDIO 40bl; Africa Studio 43tl, 43tr, 60t, 64b; Eskymaks 43br; MaraZe 43bl; gori910a 44r; Sea Wave 44l; HandmadePictures 45r, 53bl; mythja 45l; Justyna Kaminska 47br; Sokor Space 47t; tag2016 47bl; Bukhta Ihor 48tr; Thanatip S. 48b; baibaz 51tl; Elena Schweitzer 51b, 208; Oksana Shufrych 51tr; Haurylik, Alena 53tr; Krasula 53br; Natalia Mylova 53tl; casanisa 54t & 123, 57, 69br, 84–85 ; SewCream 54b & back cover top left; Auhustsinovich 59tl; HelloRF Zcool 59br; neil langan 59tr; Reschme 59bl; Iakov Filimonov 60br; SpeedKingz 60bl; Leszek Glasner 64t; Gemenacom 67; sirtravelalot 69t; thefoodphotographer 69bl, 134, 137; zarzamora 73, 75 & back cover bottom left; Oleksandra Naumenko 78; Natalia Klenova 81; Teri Virbickis 87; AnastasiaKopa 89; Elena Veselova 90; Saharosa40 97; Losangela 101, 104; bitt24 103; DronG 107; zoryanchik 109; Lyudmila Mikhailovskaya 115; Nataliya Arzamasova 144, 149, 176; Josie Grant 164& back cover bottom right; Cesarz 189; pingpongcat 192; Amallia Eka 202, 219; Elena Demyanko 205; Elena Lapshina 211; Katalin Barta 213; zstock 215; SUPERGAL 221; Rimma Bondarenko 150–51; and small watercolour illustrations throughout: Paket, AmamiArt, Le Panda.

SUPERFOODS
RECIPES&PREPARATION

Saskia Fraser

FLAME TREE
PUBLISHING

CONTENTS

INTRODUCTION

What is a superfood? Superfood is the term given to a fresh and dried edible ingredient that contains more-than-average proportions of health-promoting nutrients. Some of these 'super' foods you probably already eat without realizing just how good they are for you, while others may be brand new to you.

HOW TO USE THIS BOOK

This book is here to help you navigate the world of superfoods so that you can introduce them as part of a healthy diet for ultimate health and wellbeing. By incorporating more of these foods into your everyday lifestyle, you can supercharge your diet to help improve your mental alertness and energy levels, to help you

balance blood sugar and achieve a healthy weight, reducing niggling ailments along the way.

The prospect of using superfoods may initially seem daunting, but it is in fact easy and fun. In the following pages, you will get the lowdown on these super-healthy foods (and why they are so good for you), as well as discovering how to use them in your everyday cooking.

I have included recipes to tantalize your taste buds as well as boost your immunity and mood. Some are super-simple, while others are perfect for impressing your friends at a dinner party. Starting your day right is incredibly important for health, and you will find a great selection of smoothies and breakfasts to kickstart your day. I have included a delicious spread of simple superfood soup, salad and snack recipes to energize you too. Many of these recipes are perfect for taking to work, so you can boost your vitality, mental clarity and focus throughout the day.

Breads, bakes and sweet treats are usually made from refined ingredients that we find hard to resist. Eating them piles on the weight, saps energy and suppresses the immune system. So, here I am providing you with mouthwatering alternatives made from superfood ingredients.

These recipes not only give you a nutrient boost, but also provide a super-healthy alternative when those sweet- and carb-craving urges hit. Made with healthy sugars, complex carbohydrates and complete proteins, these breads, bakes and treats are more satisfying than the refined and processed kind, without the energy dip or bloated after-effect.

Have fun with superfoods. Mix them up, sprinkle them on and stir them in! Healthy cooking should be about maximum nutrition, ultimate tastiness and minimum fuss for all the family, so enjoy exploring these recipes and discovering more about superfoods.

A SUPER DIET

WHAT IS A SUPERFOOD?

SUPERFOOD THEORY

The concept of superfoods has been around since the early 1990s. The term is said to have been coined by the author Michael van Straten in his book titled *Superfoods*. Over the years, there has been controversy surrounding the idea of 'super' foods, as little scientific research has been undertaken to back up the theory, and many think it has been used simply as a marketing gimmick.

On the other hand, there are foods that contain relatively high amounts of certain nutrients compared with other foods, and they can be added to your shopping basket for a fun and easy way to achieve a healthier diet.

SUPERFOOD OR SUPER-FAD?

Superfoods have become highly fashionable in recent years. They are used to market everything from a smoothie to the veggies you serve for dinner, to a sugar-free snack at your local health food store. Models and actors are proponents. Turmeric shots and quinoa superfood salads are becoming more available, but is this just another fad or are superfoods here to stay?

There is little doubt that increasing the quantity of clean, wholefood ingredients in your diet will benefit your health. Simply, the more you add in these healthy foods, the more you decrease the ratio of unhealthy foods and increase the good nutrients your body has access to.

SUPER SCIENCE OR SUPER HYPE?

So, should you believe all the hype about superfoods?

Over recent years, there has been much research carried out into the nutrient content of specific wholefood ingredients. While the term 'superfood' may be controversial, there is mounting evidence to show that some foods contain particularly high traces of nutrients considered important to human health. The more we can eat of these nutrient-dense foods, the more certain we can be of fuelling our bodies in the best way possible. Much of our health is in our own hands, and taking action to boost your vitamin and mineral intake through the food you eat can be very satisfying.

WHICH FOODS ARE SUPER?

There are various ideas about what makes a food 'super' or not. In some circles, people will tell you that superfoods are powdered, high-concentrate plants and herbs, such as algae, grasses, berries, roots and mushrooms. Others will say that superfoods are certain everyday vegetables, fruits, grains, nuts and pulses that pack a nutrient punch. As there is no official scientific definition for 'superfood', you can read the evidence and make up your own mind as to which foods will benefit you the most. In a super-healthy diet, there is a place for both specialist powdered superfoods as well as the ones available in your local supermarket or grocery store.

SUPERFOOD FUN

On the whole, the term 'superfood' refers to plant-based wholefoods that contain relatively high amounts of antioxidants, essential fatty acids, vitamins and minerals, as well as other important nutrients.

Eating the colours of the rainbow through fruits and vegetables will help to ensure that you are getting a wide variety of these important powerhouses. Blue and purple foods tend to be high in antioxidants (which help prevent or stop cell damage), while green foods are high in chlorophyll (which also has antioxidant properties and is linked to natural cancer prevention).

When it comes to carbohydrate foods, some are better for you than others. Cutting out wheat and white rice and learning how to cook with grains such as quinoa will help to boost your energy and your nutrient intake.

SUPER ANIMAL PRODUCTS

Certain fish, meat and dairy products are considered by many to be highly beneficial superfoods. Oily fish such as salmon and sardines, offal (organ meats such as liver and kidneys), bone broth (a kind of rich stock), eggs, raw or fermented milk products (such as kefir) and quality animal fats (such as grass-fed butter) can be used as part of a nutrient-dense diet to improve health and wellbeing.

These foods are often considered good for brain function and joint health. There are, however, other health considerations to take into account with these food groups, such as heavy metals in fish and traces of antibiotics in meat and dairy products.

If you would like to incorporate superfood animal products into your diet, it is important to source wild fish (non-farmed) and organic/grass-fed meat, egg and dairy products – for optimum nutrition as well as to ensure the best welfare possible for the animals.

SUPERFOOD SAFETY

Chocolate

Too much of a good thing can become a bad thing. For example, chocolate has started to be spoken about as a superfood. While cocoa contains relatively high amounts of polyphenol, an antioxidant thought to play an important role in protecting our cells from oxidation, most chocolate is sweetened with unhealthy amounts of sugar. Cocoa also contains theobromine, a chemical which has similar detrimental effects on the body to caffeine.

Consuming chocolate in small amounts, made with unrefined sweeteners, allows you to take advantage of the health benefits while limiting any harmful effects.

Maca

Maca powder, an ancient herbal remedy from the mountains of Peru made from a dried root, is commonly considered a superfood. Maca is often used successfully to ease challenging symptoms of menopause and menstruation. However, because of its natural hormone-regulating properties, it is recommended that maca should not be taken alongside hormone treatments, such as hormone replacement therapy, as it may interfere with the drugs' effects.

Fruit

Consumption of too much fruit, even so-called super-fruits such as blueberries and pomegranates, can unbalance the gut and cause digestive discomfort. As a general rule, I suggest that you eat no more than 2–4 servings of fruit per day.

So, as always, the key message to take away is that the best way to eat any superfood is as part of a healthy balanced diet.

WORK-A-DAY SUPERFOODS

There are certain ingredients that you may not think of as superfoods and yet use every day. Salt, essential to the human body, is a great example of this. However, not all salt is created equal. Standard table salt is not actually very good for you. Not only do we generally consume too much of it, but it also has the important trace minerals washed out of it to make it white and often contains anti-caking additives.

Salt in its natural form, unrefined and without additives, contains a delicate and important balance of trace minerals. Overconsumption of salt is traditionally linked to high blood pressure, but ancient Indian Ayurvedic medicine prescribes unrefined sea salt to rebalance blood pressure, whether it is too low or too high. Unrefined sea salt or rock salt consumed in moderation can improve health as part of a balanced diet.

What is the difference between sea salt and rock salt? Sea salt is essentially salt that has been created from the evaporation of current sea water and then harvested, while rock salt was created as seas evaporated millions of years ago, and is mined from the land. Thus, rock salts were formed at a time when our seas did not contain the pollution that they do today – hence the popularity of rock salts, such as pink Himalayan salt, which are said to promote health.

SUPER POWERS

SUPER HEALERS

By adopting a superfood-rich diet, you could be going a long way towards avoiding or easing many illnesses and life-threatening diseases. Many people advocate the reduction of so-called acid-causing foods, such as sugar, caffeine, dairy products and gluten, which are said to create an acidic 'ash' in the body once they have been metabolized. While the science of this theory is debated, reducing your intake of 'acid-causing' foods and increasing 'alkalizing' superfoods may aid in producing a healthier environment for your cells to heal and regenerate.

Proponents argue that alkalizing your body has the potential to reduce inflammation, lowering the risk of heart disease, cancer, arthritis, skin conditions and many other diseases that may be linked to over-acidity. It is also said to boost your immune system, meaning that you are less likely to suffer from colds, flu and gastric bugs.

So, which superfoods are great for alkalizing your system, boosting your immune system and reducing disease? Some of the best alkalizing, anti-inflammatory foods include dark leafy greens, such as kale, broccoli, spinach and spirulina, as well as avocado, unrefined salt, pomegranate and coconut.

A note of caution: it is possible to over-alkalize your body if you eat only alkaline-forming foods, so aim for introducing more of these foods rather than only eating alkalizing foods.

SUPER BALANCERS

Hormone imbalance is becoming increasingly common; from hypo- and hyperthyroidism to diabetes, acne and premenstrual syndrome, most of us know someone who suffers from hormone-related problems.

Not many people realize that diet plays a role in hormonal imbalance, and it is said that the modern fashion for low-fat foods is partly to blame. Healthy fats are essential for our bodies to create hormones, so making sure we eat plenty of these important nutrients is crucial for health. Coconut oil, chia seeds, flaxseeds, coconut, extra virgin coconut oil and avocados are all sources of healthy fats.

When looking to address health issues through diet, it is just as important to think about cutting out unhealthy foods as it is to think about introducing health-boosting

foods. Processed foods contain many refined ingredients that could hinder hormone health.

Hormone imbalance is also closely linked to gut health, therefore foods that are said to heal and balance the digestive system may help to heal the endocrine (hormone) system. To help rebalance your hormonal system naturally, try including plenty of superfood ingredients that are good for the gut, such as spices like turmeric and ginger, soothing bone broths and probiotic live foods such as kefir and kimchi.

SUPER DETOXERS

Our bodies are naturally detoxing all the time, removing toxins through the elimination systems and maintaining the homeostasis required for life. Some people think that detoxification diets and protocols are a waste of time, but for anyone who has ever done a detox, you will know just how much better you feel afterwards. When doing a

health-boosting detox, it is normal for energy and brain function to increase, aches and pains to decrease, skin to become clear and smooth, eyes to sparkle and moods to become more balanced. When your system is clean, you experience a general sense of wellbeing, both physically and emotionally.

The best way to help your body detox is by aiming to eat a clean and healthy diet every day, but certain superfoods can assist in drawing toxins out of the body. Regularly consuming these 'super detoxers' helps your body to eliminate unwanted waste products that have been stored in cells, often causing fatigue, brain fog, aches and pains.

If you would love more energy and to feel more alert, smoothies and freshly made juices are wonderful cleansers, as are dark green vegetables such as kale, broccoli, spinach and chard. Other super detoxers include green tea, garlic, mung beans, citrus fruits and beetroot (beets).

SUPER MOOD ENHANCERS

Feeling low, irritable or overwhelmed can sometimes successfully be alleviated through a change in diet. Most of us manage our energy artificially – using caffeine and sugar to increase energy and carbohydrates and alcohol to relax – which can cause hypoglycaemia. Many people suffer unknowingly from hypoglycaemia – low blood sugar – which lessens one's ability to deal with stress, as well as contributing to mood swings and irritability.

Blood sugar can be rebalanced through eating a cleaner diet and managing energy levels naturally through enough sleep and hydration. Consuming certain superfoods on a regular basis has the potential to enhance your mood and keep you feeling more emotionally balanced, even during stressful times. To rebalance blood sugar levels naturally, avoid processed foods and anything containing processed fats, white flour, sugar and potatoes. Instead, eat a balanced diet rich in superfood proteins,

such as nuts, eggs and salmon, superfood slow-release carbohydrates like quinoa, oats and sweet potatoes, and plenty of superfood greens, such as broccoli, kale and spirulina. Other ingredients that are particularly good for balancing blood sugar include cinnamon, chia seeds and extra virgin coconut oil.

Note:

Deficiencies in iron, vitamin D and essential fatty acids can also contribute to depression and brain fog.

SUPER SKIN

The state of our skin, hair and eyes reflect the state of our internal health – they are the mirrors to our insides. Severe skin problems as well as dull skin, open pores and yellowish eyes can often be improved by eating a clean diet containing plenty of superfoods. When your system is clean, you look younger and fresher as your skin

clears up and becomes firmer, your cheeks glow, the whites of your eyes become whiter and your hair regains its lustre. You seem to shine from the inside out.

Skin issues, such as acne and eczema, are often caused by toxins in the system, after years of eating a less-than-optimum diet, as well as allergies and poor gut health. Common food intolerances that sometimes cause skin conditions include dairy products, refined sugar and gluten.

Removing these from your diet has the potential to make a big difference. Certain foods are particularly good for skin health, including avocados, red and yellow peppers, oily fish such as sardines and mackerel, and greens such as broccoli and kale.

You can also have fun using home-made skin and hair treatments, which can contain superfoods such as oats, coconut oil and honey to cleanse and heal the skin and condition hair naturally.

SUPER WEIGHT LOSS

Many of us carry more weight than we would like. Our lives are stressful and busy and it is easy to grab unhealthy foods and eat too much when we are rushed off our feet. By eating a cleaner diet and introducing more healthy superfoods, you can turn the tide on feeling overweight and sluggish and increase your metabolism, boosting your body's natural ability to lose weight.

In recent dieting paradigms, fat has been seen as the bad boy of weight loss. While it is true that highly processed fats and oils are bad for health, recent research has shown that healthy fats are, in fact, essential for maintaining an efficient metabolism, which in turn is essential for maintaining a healthy weight. To aid with weight loss, try cooking with extra virgin coconut oil and include it in your smoothies. Add avocados to your salads and lunch boxes and snack on raw seeds and nuts instead of crisps (potato chips) and cookies.

Replacing white carbohydrates with superfood carbohydrates can also contribute greatly to weight loss. Replace white potatoes, wheat pasta and white rice with super-healthy alternatives such as sweet potatoes, buckwheat noodles and quinoa and you may well begin to notice a difference.

SUPER BRAIN BOOSTERS

Brain fog, poor memory and unclear thinking seem to get worse as we age. While this decline in brain function is usually put down to 'getting older', it is often possible to reverse the trend. Brain fog has been linked to toxicity and so there is the potential to regain sharp thinking and a good memory simply by eating a cleaner diet rich in brain-boosting superfoods.

Essential fatty acids, protein and blood sugar balance all play a part in healthy brain function. Increase your essential fatty acid and protein intake by eating superfoods such as salmon, mackerel and sardines, chia seeds, flaxseeds, walnuts and Brazil nuts. Help to rebalance blood sugar by cutting out processed foods and eating a wholefood diet with superfood carbohydrates.

Being well hydrated is also essential for good brain function. If you begin to suffer from brain fog or unclear thinking, try drinking a large glass of water, then wait five minutes and if you notice yourself brightening up, your poor brain function may simply be down to dehydration. Mineralizing your drinking water by adding a small amount of unrefined salt – about one pinch per gallon (*c.* 4 litres) – can enhance your body's ability to absorb the water, therefore improving brain function more rapidly.

THE SUPERHEROES

Superfood ingredients are easy to come by, either in your local supermarket, grocery or health food store. But which foods are superfoods, what are they supposed to be good for and how do you use them?

The various groups of superfoods offer different nutrient properties and, when eaten as part of a healthy diet, have the potential to change your health profile dramatically. Consuming a broad range of superfoods will give you the best chance of getting all the nutrients you need for energy, mental wellbeing and physical fitness. Understand a little more about these superheroes of the food world.

SUPER FRUITS

Summer Berries

Summer berries (such as blueberries, blackberries, strawberries, raspberries, redcurrants and blackcurrants) are loaded with vitamin C and antioxidants, which are said to be anti-ageing and able to help fight common diseases. They are also low on the glycaemic index, so good for people on low-sugar diets. Blueberries are particularly 'super', as their blue skin colour means they contain high levels of the antioxidant anthocyanin.

Goji Berries

Not only do they have a unique fudge-like flavour and red-orange colour, goji berries are little powerhouses of nutrition. They are high in protein, vitamin C, beta carotene and iron, useful in aiding detoxification and for reducing inflammation. Eat them dried, or for a sweeter flavour, soak for a few hours in fresh water.

Mulberries

Mulberries are said to help boost immunity, increase iron levels and aid digestion. Fresh mulberries are hard to find, but dried mulberries are readily available in health food stores. They have a caramel-like flavour and chewy texture – great for snacking and for adding to breakfast bowls, smoothies and salads.

Pomegranate

The juicy red seeds of pomegranates are a good source of antioxidants, important in reducing inflammation and with the potential to soothe gut diseases and arthritis. High in vitamins, particularly vitamin C, the juice from pomegranate seeds also helps to boost the immune system.

Coconut

The flesh and hydrating water in coconuts both contain an abundance of essential nutrients. Coconut oil is one of the most stable oils for cooking and may help with weight loss, heart health and reducing high blood pressure.

SUPER GREENS

Broccoli

Studies have shown that adding broccoli's powerful antioxidant mix to your diet could reduce the potential for heart disease and age-related eye disease, as well as increasing bone strength. It is a member of the Cruciferae family, which, as part of a healthy diet, may be of benefit to people with cancer.

Seaweed

Seaweed is a source of protein as well as essential fatty acids and B vitamins. Rich in minerals such as calcium, copper, iodine and iron, introducing seaweeds such as nori, dulse, arame, hijiki, wakame and kombu into your diet may help improve brain function, reduce inflammation and balance hormones.

Kale

Kale is the king when it comes to leafy greens. Types of kale include curly kale, Russian kale and cavolo nero (black or Tuscan kale) – all powerhouses of phytonutrients and chlorophyll, thought to be good for everything from weight loss to fighting cancer. Kale is also a good source of potassium and iron.

Wheatgrass & Barley Grass

Wheatgrass and barley grass are said to be highly alkalizing, with the potential to reduce inflammation in the body. Introduce these superfood grasses into your diet in juice form, drunk as a single shot or added to fresh fruit juice, or in powdered form added to smoothies and breakfast bowls.

SUPER VEGGIES

Beetroot (Beet)

In traditional Chinese medicine, beetroot is considered a blood cleanser. Its red colour contains powerful antioxidants, and its leaves are rich in calcium and iron. Eat them in soups, grated into salads and roasted.

Sweet Potatoes

Sweet potatoes are high in the antioxidant beta carotene and contain iron, calcium and vitamin C. Sweet potatoes are delicious boiled, mashed and roasted, as well as being a good addition to soups.

Tomatoes

Tomatoes are a rich source of vitamins C and A, iron, potassium and antioxidants such as lycopene and beta carotene, which may help to defend against cancer and other diseases. Enjoy them in salads, salsas, wraps and soups.

Avocados

Avocados are a wonderful source of healthy fats, as well as vitamin E. Healthy fats are important for weight loss, supple skin, healthy joints and brain function. Try adding half an avocado to smoothies for extra creaminess.

Onions

Onions have been traditionally used for the relief of coughs, colds and asthma. For a simple but effective cough syrup, soak half a raw onion in honey. Take a teaspoon of the onion-infused honey to ease coughing.

Mung Bean Sprouts

Mung bean sprouts are high in protein and low in fat, containing essential minerals such as manganese and copper, and vitamins C and K. Find them in supermarkets or grocery stores and use them in stir-fries and salads.

SUPER POWDERS

Açaí

Açaí (pronounced 'ah-sa-EE') berries are said to be even higher in anti-ageing, disease-fighting antioxidants than blueberries and goji berries. Although they grow fresh on palm trees in Latin America, you will most commonly find them in dry powdered form. Add a teaspoon or two for a delicious addition to smoothies and breakfast bowls.

Lucuma

Lucuma fruit come from the Andes and are grown in Peru, Ecuador and Chile. The fruit powder has a maple syrup-like taste and may help to maintain balanced blood sugar. It is a good source of antioxidants and vitamins and is a wonderful addition to desserts and smoothies.

Blue Green Algae

Blue green algae, such as spirulina and chlorella, grows in freshwater lakes. Algae contains the complete spectrum of essential amino acids as well as a huge number of vitamins and minerals. It has a strong flavour that is an acquired taste, so start with a small amount, adding ¼ to 1 teaspoon of powder to smoothies and breakfast bowls.

Maca

Maca is a Peruvian root vegetable belonging to the Cruciferae family. It has been used for centuries as a traditional herbal remedy for treating hormonal issues, including skin conditions, menstrual and menopausal problems, and as an aphrodisiac. Add 1–2 tablespoons to your breakfast smoothies.

Top left clockwise from top: Wheat grass, spirulina, cacao, lucuma, goji, and maca powders;
Top right: Açai powder and berries; Bottom left: Chlorella powder;
Bottom right: Maca powder and a maca shake

SUPER PROTECTORS

Cocoa

Cocoa has one of the most impressive arrays of antioxidants – the great protector nutrients – of any food, and is most commonly found in chocolate. It is also a rich source of minerals, including magnesium. When buying chocolate, choose brands made with healthy sugars. Add unsweetened cocoa to desserts, cakes and smoothies.

Green Tea

Green tea is also high in cell-protecting antioxidants. It may help to speed up metabolism, aiding with weight loss and improving brain function. Green tea comes in various forms, with fine-powdered matcha green tea working best in food recipes. It is a good alternative to coffee, containing a much smaller amount of caffeine.

SUPER HERBS

Rosemary

Rosemary is a woody herb that can be eaten raw or cooked. Its pungent smell comes from numerous plant oils, which are said to be antimicrobial, antifungal and anti-inflammatory. Rosemary has been used to enhance health for centuries, through cooking with the herb or using the extracted oil essences.

Oregano

Oregano is a Mediterranean herb that is widely used in Italian and Greek cooking. Oregano oil has traditionally been used as a herbal medicine to treat intestinal parasites, yeast infections and skin conditions. Add the leafy herb, dried or fresh, liberally to pasta dishes, soups and salads.

Parsley

Parsley is one of the most potent green salad herbs. There is strong evidence that parsley is anti-inflammatory, good for bone strengthening, reducing water retention and balancing blood sugar. To reap the full benefits of this amazing herb, add it generously to smoothies, salads and pasta dishes.

Mint

Mint is a wonderful digestive, thought to enhance bile secretion, aiding digestion and helping to ease stomach problems and discomfort after eating. Drink it as a herbal tea, add it to smoothies, fruit salads and Middle-Eastern style salads, and use a mint-infused foot bath to relieve swollen and tired feet.

SUPER SPICES

Spices have been used medicinally in the Far and Middle East to boost immunity and fight disease for millennia. Benefit from the health-giving properties of these powerful seasonings by using them in your everyday cooking.

Garlic

OK, it's not a spice as such, but, similarly to spices, we use it for its pungent flavour. And its pungency translates into other powers too: from the common cold to fungal infections, people use this incredible ingredient to relieve symptoms and increase health all over the world. Its antiseptic, antifungal and antimicrobial properties are most potent when eaten raw.

Ginger & Turmeric

Ginger and turmeric both have strong soothing and warming properties. Ginger is amazing for nausea and stomach aches, while turmeric is an incredible anti-inflammatory. Infuse them (individually or together; up to one tablespoon each, if using fresh, or one teaspoon, if dried) in boiling water to make a soothing tea.

Cinnamon

Despite the sweet taste of cinnamon, it contains no sugar and actually balances blood sugar. It is delicious added to porridge (oatmeal), smoothies and desserts, as well as added to Middle Eastern stews.

Cloves

Cloves are antifungal, antibacterial, antiseptic and analgesic and have traditionally been used for toothache, intestinal cleansing, rheumatism and respiratory infections. Cloves can be added to cooking or infused to make a delicious and warming tea.

Cayenne

Cayenne peppers are a type of chili pepper, used therapeutically throughout the world. Among many other symptoms, cayenne pepper has been used to calm digestive disorders, clear congestion and prevent migraines. Add it to soups, stir-fries and stews.

SUPER SEEDS

Superfood seeds come in many shapes and sizes. They all contain the essential building blocks to grow into much larger plants, packing the dense mix of nutrients required for this amazing process.

Hemp Seeds

Hemp seeds are a rich source of plant protein and essential fatty acids, making them a great addition to any store cupboard. They can be eaten whole or bought hulled and added to breakfasts, smoothies and salads.

Flaxseeds & Chia Seeds

The modern diet contains a disproportionate amount of omega-6 fatty acids. Eating flax- and chia seeds can begin to address this imbalance, as they contain high levels of omega 3. Add them to smoothies, breakfasts and desserts. (Flaxseeds are also known as linseeds.)

Sesame & Pumpkin Seeds

Essential fatty acids are abundant in sesame and pumpkin seeds, as well as magnesium and calcium – great for good sleep and strong bones. They are delicious raw or toasted, added to salads and sprinkled over breakfast.

Quinoa & Buckwheat

Quinoa and buckwheat are often mistaken for grains, but are in fact non-grass plant seeds that are consumed like grains, and are much healthier for you than real cereal (grass) grains. Both are sources of whole protein, and are said to help reduce inflammation and stabilize blood sugar.

Top left: Hulled hemp seeds, Top right: Chia seeds, flaxseeds and white and black sesame seeds,
Bottom: Red, black and white quinoa seeds

SUPER PROTEINS

Oily Fish

Oily fish such as salmon, mackerel and sardines are known to support good health. They are a rich source of omega-3 fatty acids, vitamin D and selenium, said to guard against cardiovascular disease and dementia.

Eggs

Eggs have been a staple part of the human diet for millennia. They are an inexpensive source of high-quality protein, containing a rich mix of vitamins and minerals.

Brazil Nuts

Brazil nuts are the best-known selenium food source in the world. Selenium is essential for a healthy immune system and low levels have been linked to depression, tiredness and anxiety. Brazils are a delicious snack.

Walnuts

Walnuts are a rich source of the all-important omega-3 fatty acids. They are delicious raw and roasted and can be used in a wide variety of recipes as a protein-rich addition.

Bee Pollen

This is the pollen harvested by bees. It is high in protein, as well as other antioxidants and vitamins (it will give you a good supply of B vitamins, including B12). Sprinkle bee pollen on your breakfast, desserts and smoothies. Hayfever sufferers should be cautious and start with very small amounts. If no reaction has occurred within 24 hours, then they may find that it even helps alleviate allergy symptoms in the long run.

Pulses

Pulses (such as dried beans, chickpeas and lentils) are a rich source of folate, iron, calcium, magnesium, zinc and potassium. Low in calories and high in complex carbohydrates, they are good for weight loss and for balancing blood sugar.

Bone Broth

Bone broths are cooked for longer than traditional stocks, releasing important nutrients from within the bones. They are rich in minerals, collagen, glutamine, glycine and proline, which may help to heal the gut lining and reduce inflammation.

SUPER LIVE

Live fermented foods are said to be one of the best promoters of gut health. They are natural probiotics, aiding a strong immune system and helping to avoid disease and boost recovery.

Kefir

Kefir is a fermented drink made from milk that helps healthy gut bacteria to thrive. To prepare kefir, special 'grains' are added to milk – these are a 'mother' culture of bacterial and yeast strains which ferment the milk – or a powdered bacterial starter can be used. You can also get a water version of kefir.

You can make kefir yourself at home or buy it from health food stores. Add it to smoothies and breakfasts.

Top: Bone broth
Bottom: Kefir and kefir grains

Kombucha

Kombucha is a live fermented drink made with a starter known as a 'scoby'. Natural flavourings are added for extra nutrient-richness and taste. Find kombucha in health food stores, or buy a home-brew starter kit online.

Sauerkraut

Sauerkraut's sour taste and health-giving properties come from pickling finely sliced cabbage with salt and naturally occurring airborne lactic acid bacteria. It is easy to make at home and is available in health food stores.

Kimchi

Korean kimchi can be made with a variety of vegetables, but traditionally contains Chinese (napa) cabbage and Korean radishes. The addition of ingredients such as chili pepper, ginger and garlic give it a wonderful depth of flavour.

Yogurt

Yogurt contains the most health-promoting live bacteria when it has been fermented for at least 24 hours, so have a go at making your own with organic cows', goats' or coconut milk.

Kimchi

SUPER GRAINS

Oats

Oats are naturally gluten-free and a source of complex carbohydrates, helping to balance blood sugar and alleviate symptoms of gluten intolerance. Oats contain high amounts of dietary fibre and are reported to have cholesterol-lowering properties. A cautionary note: oats are often processed alongside gluten-containing grains, so may contain mild traces of gluten.

Freekeh

Freekeh is derived from young, green durum wheat. It has a protein content higher than quinoa and is low on the glycaemic index, making it a good option for diabetics and for weight loss. Although freekeh is not gluten-free, it is a delicious and healthy alternative to white rice and pasta.

Farro

Farro, also known as emmer, comes from the same wheat grain strain as spelt and einkorn. This ancient grain is said to be easier to digest and contains less gluten than modern wheat varieties. Farro is traditionally used in Italian cooking and is more nutritionally dense than modern wheat.

Sorghum

Sorghum is a gluten-free grain that can be used as a rice substitute or, as flour, in baking. It has a similar nutrient profile to oats and can be used as part of a low-glycaemic diet for weight loss and blood sugar balance. Its high fibre content means that it is also good for bowel health.

Clockwise from top left: Oats, freekeh, farro and sorghum

GETTING THE MOST FROM SUPERFOODS

Most superfoods contain essential vitamins, minerals and phytonutrients that are damaged or reduced by extended cooking times and poor storage. In this chapter, we look at where to get your superfoods, ways to maintain their nutrient content and the best kitchen equipment to use so you can reap the most benefit from these powerhouses of nutrition.

SOURCING

Finding good sources for buying your superfoods makes life a lot easier, whether it be that special veg shop that sells organic veggies, or that Ebay seller who does great superfood powders. Superfoods can be expensive, so shop around to find the best deals both locally and online.

Fresh Foods

Sourcing fresh organic fruits and vegetables can be simple if you have easy access to markets, supermarkets or grocery stores with a good organic selection. However, if you prefer not to shop at supermarkets or you live rurally, get a weekly veg box delivery from a company that allows you to order specific fresh superfood ingredients.

Dried Foods

Pretty much all dried superfoods can be bought online, and are often better value when ordered through the internet. More everyday dried superfoods, such as oats, lentils and quinoa, will be readily available from your local health food store or supermarket. Shop around to find the supplier with the best deals.

STORING

Fresh Foods

Fresh fruits and vegetables will maintain more of their nutrient content and last longer
if stored correctly. To keep vegetables fresh, make sure they are dry and store
them in a plastic bag or airtight container in the refrigerator. Wrap herbs loosely
in newspaper or kitchen paper and keep them in the refrigerator. Store berries
uncovered in the refrigerator. Keep fresh fish in an airtight container in the refrigerator
and eat within a few days of purchasing or by the 'use-by' (expiration) date on the
packaging. Keep fresh eggs in the refrigerator. Leave unripe fruit uncovered at room
temperature to ripen.

Dried Foods

Many dried superfoods contain volatile nutrients that degrade when exposed to
air. For this reason, it is important to keep them in airtight containers, and all dried
superfoods will benefit from being kept out of direct sunlight. Superfoods with
important fats, such as cold-pressed coconut oil, hemp oil, nuts and seeds, will do
better when kept in the refrigerator. The longer these ingredients are kept at room
temperature, or exposed to the damaging rays of the sun, the more quickly their
sensitive oils will degrade and become rancid. Discard dried superfoods that have
lost their taste or smell.

COOKING METHODS

Cooking with superfoods is easy, but knowing a few basic rules will help to protect delicate nutrients from degrading during the cooking process. Avoid overcooking, as extended periods of exposure to heat will destroy antioxidants, vitamins and phytonutrients. Avoid using refined vegetable oils and choose cold-pressed oils instead.

Vegetables

There are many ways to cook superfood vegetables. To retain the most goodness, avoid overcooking. The most nutrient-efficient way to cook vegetables is by steaming. If you want to sauté or stir-fry, use coconut oil or 'water fry' with a few tablespoons of water. To roast or bake vegetables, use coconut oil or extra virgin olive oil.

Grains & Seeds

Cooking with superfood grains, such as farro, and superfood seeds, like quinoa, is simple and quick when you know how. As a general rule, whatever volume of grain you use, use double the volume of water; bring to the boil, reduce to a simmer and cook for approximately 10 minutes until the water has been absorbed.

Oily Fish

The healthiest way to prepare oily fish from fresh is to bake or poach it in the oven, or cook it in a steamer. To maintain as many nutrients as possible, be careful not to overcook the fish – it should be just cooked through but still tender and juicy.

COLD PREPARATION METHODS

Many superfoods can be eaten uncooked. Eating fresh fruits and vegetables as well as superfood powders in their raw state helps to retain the maximum number of nutrients possible. Fresh smoothies and salads have become very popular among health-conscious people for good reason – they help to make you feel great!

Fruits

Super-fruits should be eaten when fully ripe for the best nutritional advantage. Not only do they taste sweeter and more flavourful, they provide the most energy and nutrient content too. Use superfood fruit powders, such as lucuma and açaí, in small quantities because of their intense flavours and condensed nutrient content.

Nuts & Seeds

Most superfood nuts and seeds will benefit from being soaked overnight. This releases enzyme inhibitors that keep the nut or seed in its dormant state. Once soaked, their nutrient content expands rapidly as they begin the journey to becoming a plant.

Note:

The fragile oils in nuts and seeds are degraded by cooking.

Herbs

Fresh and dried super-herbs are a wonderful addition to any meal. If using fresh herbs, bruise the leaves by rubbing them between your fingers before finely chopping and adding to cold or cooked dishes. Dried herbs benefit from at least 10 minutes of cooking to fully release their flavours.

KiTCHEN EQUiPMENT

Making superfood dishes does not require specialist equipment, but there are some basic kitchen items that will help to retain nutrients, promote health and speed up preparation. Having the right kitchen kit makes cooking a lot more fun, and expands the scope of recipes that you can try.

Preparation

A good blender and food processor will make creating superfood dishes easy and quick. A hand blender will suffice, but a higher-speed jug blender and a dedicated food processor will make life much easier. Think of these bits of kitchen equipment as an investment in your long-term health.

Cooking

Standard kitchen saucepans and utensils will serve for most superfood recipes. A tiered steamer pan is useful when cooking vegetables. Cooking with damaged nonstick pans can potentially leach harmful chemicals into food, so use nonstick pans in good condition. Aluminium pans and utensils have been linked to Alzheimer's disease, so are best avoided.

Storing

When exposed to the air, all foods begin to degrade (through the process of oxidization). Airtight storage containers will help to retain nutrients and keep any prepared food fresh for longer. There is some concern that toxins from plastic can leach into food, so invest in stainless steel and glass storage containers when you can.

BREAKFASTS & SMOOTHIES

AÇAÍ SMOOTHIE BOWL

Freezing is a great way to use up ripe bananas. Simply peel them, cut them into chunks and pop them in a freezer bag. Blend them mixed into smoothies or alone for a super-healthy dairy-free alternative to ice cream.

Makes 1 bowl

2 frozen bananas

2 handfuls blueberries

1 tsp açaí powder

100 ml/3½ fl oz/⅓ cup water

2 tsp chia seeds

1 tsp bee pollen

Blend the frozen bananas, blueberries, açaí powder and water until smooth and creamy. Pour into a bowl and top with chia seeds and bee pollen. Serve immediately.

COCONUT MILK CHIA BOWL

I have suggested blueberries and nectarine for the topping in this recipe, but you can use whatever fruit you happen to have at home. If you like experimenting with recipes, try flavouring the chia porridge with cinnamon or vanilla.

Makes 1 bowl

200 ml/7 fl oz/¾ cup canned coconut milk
100 ml/3½ fl oz/⅓ cup warm water
3 tbsp chia seeds
1 tsp maple syrup or runny honey

For the topping

fresh fruit of your choice, such as blueberries and nectarine
fresh coconut (optional)

Mix the coconut milk, water, chia seeds and maple syrup or honey together in a breakfast bowl, making sure that the chia seeds are evenly distributed throughout the liquid.

Leave for 30–60 minutes or overnight in the refrigerator, so that the chia seeds swell and thicken into a porridge.

Top with fresh fruit and coconut before eating.

OATIE BREAKFAST BARS

These bars are delicious any time of day, but are particularly good with a cup of coffee or herbal tea for breakfast. For a variation, try replacing the blueberries with raspberries or apple.

Makes 6-8 bars

For the base

coconut oil, for greasing

4 ripe bananas

2 tsp ground cinnamon

200 g/7 oz/2 cups rolled oats

125 g/4 oz/1 cup blueberries

For the topping

25 g/1 oz/¼ cup rolled oats

25 g/1 oz/¼ cup pumpkin seeds

25 g/1 oz/¼ cup sunflower seeds

25 g/1 oz/¼ cup cashew nuts

2 tbsp chia seeds

handful puffed quinoa

2 tbsp coconut oil

1 tbsp date syrup

Preheat the oven to 180°C/350°F/Gas Mark 4. Grease a 24 x 15 cm/9½ x 6 inch baking tray (baking pan) with coconut oil.

For the base, blend or mash the bananas with the cinnamon. Mix the oats in thoroughly and spread the mixture into the baking tray. Sprinkle the blueberries evenly on top. Bake for 10 minutes.

Meanwhile, mix all the topping ingredients together in a bowl. Remove the base from the oven and sprinkle the topping evenly over the top. Bake for a further 20 minutes until golden. Allow to cool, then cut into 6–8 breakfast bars.

Store in an airtight container in the refrigerator and eat within 5 days.

BLUEBERRY YOGURT SMOOTHIE

The blueberries give this smoothie a gorgeous colour as well as a heavenly flavour. I try to avoid dairy, so I usually make this with coconut yogurt, but it works equally well with goats' or cows' yogurt.

Makes 1 large glass

4 handfuls blueberries

1 ripe banana

3 heaped dessert spoons yogurt or coconut yogurt

200 ml/7 fl oz/¾ cup water

Blend all the ingredients together until smooth and creamy.

Pour into a tall glass and drink immediately, or put it in a flask with a couple of ice cubes for drinking later.

HOMEMADE GRANOLA

Homemade granola is so much better than bought granola, in taste and health benefits. You can use any kind of dried fruit, but I love the golden hue of the apricots here.

3 tbsp extra virgin coconut oil

3 tbsp honey or maple syrup

1 tbsp ground cinnamon

2 pinches unrefined salt

1 tbsp cider vinegar

250 g/9 oz/2⅔ cups rolled oats

100 g/3½ oz/¾ cup hazelnuts

50 g/2 oz/½ cup walnuts

50 g/2 oz/⅓ cup sunflower seeds

100 g/3½ oz/¾ cup dried apricots, chopped

Preheat the oven to 150°C/300°F/Gas Mark 2.

Gently melt the coconut oil with the honey or maple syrup, cinnamon and salt in a small saucepan. Once melted, remove from the heat and stir in the vinegar.

Combine the oats, hazelnuts, walnuts and sunflower seeds in a mixing bowl. Pour on the ingredients from the saucepan and mix thoroughly with a large spoon or your hands.

Spread the granola mixture thinly and evenly over 1–2 large baking trays (baking pans). Bake for 30–45 minutes until golden, stirring every 15 minutes so that it toasts evenly.

Remove from the oven, stir in the dried apricots and allow to cool before storing in an airtight container.

MELON, CUCUMBER & GINGER SMOOTHIE

I have suggested cantaloupe or honeydew melon for this smoothie, but you can use whichever melon is in season or your favourite variety. Cucumber may seem a strange addition to a smoothie, but you'll be surprised by how well it works here.

Makes 1 large glass

⅓ melon, such as cantaloupe or honeydew, diced

¼ cucumber, diced

1 tsp very finely chopped ginger

250 ml/8 fl oz/1 cup water

Blend all the ingredients together in a blender until smooth.

Pour into a tall glass and drink immediately, or put it in a flask with a couple of ice cubes for drinking later.

KALE SMOOTHIE

Kale can be quite a strong flavour in smoothies, but you can barely taste it in this yummy drink. Surprisingly filling, it works as a superfood snack any time of day.

Makes 1 large glass

handful kale, stalks removed

2 ripe pears, cored

200 ml/7 fl oz/¾ cup unsweetened hemp milk

100 ml/3½ fl oz/⅓ cup water

small handful mint leaves

1 tsp flaxseeds

Blend all the ingredients together in a blender until smooth and creamy.

Pour into a tall glass and drink immediately, or put it in a flask with a couple of ice cubes for drinking later.

SPIRULINA COCONUT SMOOTHIE BOWL

Depending on the richness of the brand of coconut yogurt that you can find, this recipe may be enough for two breakfasts. The beautiful colours and textures of this smoothie bowl are a feast for the eyes.

Makes 1 large or 2 small bowls

250 g/9 oz/1 cup coconut yogurt
¼ tsp spirulina
1 banana

For the topping

kiwi fruit
blueberries
coconut flakes
chia seeds

Blend the yogurt, spirulina and banana together in a blender until smooth and creamy.

Pour into 1–2 bowls and add your toppings.

QUINOA PORRIDGE

The quinoa in this recipe gives you a great protein-rich start to your day. I have used mixed quinoa here, but feel free to use a single colour if that is what you have.

Serves 1

5 tbsp mixed black, brown and white quinoa

150 ml/¼ pint/⅔ cup unsweetened coconut or oat milk, plus extra to serve

1 tsp honey or maple syrup, plus extra to taste (optional)

½ banana, sliced

¼ apple, sliced

a few blueberries

small handful pecan nuts

Rinse the quinoa in a sieve (strainer) under cold running water to remove its bitter coating.

Put the quinoa, milk and honey or maple syrup in a saucepan and bring to the boil. Reduce the heat, cover and simmer for 10 minutes. Turn the heat off and leave to stand for 5 minutes.

Serve in your breakfast bowl, topped with the fruit, nuts and with an extra splash of milk and maple syrup or honey, if you like.

POWER BREAKFAST

When you want a special weekend breakfast that's full of superfood punch, this delicious power bowl of goodness hits the spot. Without eggs, it is totally vegan, with the chickpea sprouts providing ample protein.

Makes 2 breakfasts

4 handfuls mixed salad leaves

small handful mint leaves

1 green chili, finely sliced (optional)

8 cherry tomatoes, quartered

2 handfuls sprouted chickpeas

1 tbsp pumpkin seeds

½ ripe avocado, peeled and sliced

4 sundried tomato halves, chopped

2 eggs (optional)

1 tbsp olive oil (optional)

2 pinches dried chili (pepper) flakes (optional)

For the dressing (optional)

3 tbsp extra virgin olive oil

1 tbsp lime juice

½ garlic clove, peeled and crushed

¼ tsp maple syrup or honey

large pinch unrefined salt

If using, mix all the salad dressing ingredients together thoroughly and set aside.

Toss the salad leaves, mint leaves, green chili and dressing together, then divide between two breakfast bowls.

Top with the cherry tomatoes, sprouted chickpeas, pumpkin seeds, avocado and sundried tomatoes.

To fry the eggs, if using, heat the olive oil in a frying pan until hot. Crack the eggs into the pan and cook over a medium heat until the whites are just firm. Add to your breakfast bowl.

Finish with a sprinkle of chili (pepper) flakes over each bowl, if you like.

BARLEY GRASS & BANANA SMOOTHIE

Barley grass is similar to wheatgrass in nutrient content, with a more universally palatable flavour. You can replace the barley grass in this smoothie with any green superfood powder or powder mix, available in good health food stores and online.

Makes 1 large glass

2 ripe bananas
1 level tsp barley grass powder
300 ml/½ pint/1¼ cups unsweetened hemp milk

Blend all the ingredients together in a blender until smooth and creamy.

Pour into a tall glass and drink immediately, or put it in a flask with a couple of ice cubes for drinking later.

BLUEBERRY KEFIR SMOOTHIE

Buy kefir from a good health food store or try making your own. If you want to make it at home, you can buy kefir starter grains online – there are two types of kefir starter grains: those for milk and those for water. Milk kefir is classic kefir.

Makes 1 large glass

300 ml/½ pint/1¼ cups kefir (made from coconut milk or organic milk)
2 handfuls blueberries
zest of ¼ lemon
1–2 tsp honey or maple syrup, to taste

Blend all the ingredients together in a blender until smooth and creamy.

Pour into a tall glass and drink immediately, or put it in a flask with a couple of ice cubes for drinking later.

SALADS

BROCCOLI & FETA SALAD

Tomato and feta cheese is a classic Greek combination that works beautifully with broccoli. Get organic feta if you can – most major supermarkets or grocery stores and health food stores will stock it.

Serves 1 as a main or 3 as a side

100 g/3½ oz broccoli
6 cherry tomatoes, halved
handful rocket (arugula) leaves
50 g/2 oz feta cheese, crumbled

For the simple balsamic vinaigrette

2 tbsp olive oil
2 tsp balsamic vinegar
unrefined salt and freshly ground black pepper

Mix all the vinaigrette ingredients together thoroughly in a bowl, adding salt and pepper to taste. Set aside.

Steam the broccoli for 10 minutes. Rinse under cold running water to prevent the broccoli continuing to cook.

Toss the cooked broccoli with the cherry tomatoes and rocket (arugula). Sprinkle over the crumbled feta cheese and serve with the vinaigrette.

KALE BUDDHA BOWL

This beautiful Buddha bowl makes a delicious lunch or supper. If you prefer, lightly steam the kale for 5–7 minutes before making up the dish. If you can't find pea shoots, use rocket (arugula) leaves instead.

Serves 1

1 tbsp extra virgin olive oil

100 g/3½ oz butternut squash,
   peeled and diced

2 handfuls shredded kale, stalks removed

100 g/3½ oz/¾ cup canned
   chickpeas, rinsed

½ ripe avocado, peeled and sliced

pea shoots or rocket (arugula), to garnish

For the tahini dressing (optional)

1 tbsp tahini

2 tbsp olive oil

1 tbsp lemon juice

½ tsp honey or maple syrup

1 small garlic clove, peeled and crushed

unrefined salt

Heat the olive oil in a lidded saucepan over a low heat and cook the butternut squash with the lid on for 15–20 minutes, turning the squash occasionally, until tender.

Meanwhile, if using, mix all the dressing ingredients together thoroughly in a bowl, adding salt to taste. Set aside.

Lay a bed of kale and top with the cooked butternut squash, chickpeas and avocado. Drizzle over the dressing, if using, and garnish with a few pea shoots or rocket (arugula) leaves.

WARM QUINOA SALAD

This nutritious salad is a delicious addition to any meal, and is substantial enough to be a satisfying main dish on its own. For a variation, try swapping the squash for sweet potato.

Serves 1 as a main or 3 as a side

50 g/2 oz/1¼ cup tricolore quinoa, rinsed

150 g/5 oz butternut squash, peeled, seeded and diced

150 ml/1¼ pint/⅔ cup water

100 g/3½ oz small raw broccoli florets

12 baby tomatoes, halved

3 fresh thyme sprigs, leaves only

½ yellow pepper, seeded and diced

For the French vinaigrette

4 tbsp extra virgin olive oil

1 tbsp lemon juice

1 tsp Dijon mustard

½ tsp honey or maple syrup

unrefined salt

Mix all the vinaigrette ingredients together thoroughly in a bowl. Add salt to taste. Set aside.

Bring the quinoa to a boil in 150 ml/¼ pint/⅔ cup water. Reduce to a simmer and cook for 10 minutes with the lid on. Remove from the heat and leave to stand for 5 minutes.

Meanwhile, steam the butternut squash for 10 minutes until soft.

In a warmed salad bowl, toss all the salad ingredients with the vinaigrette and serve.

FRESH SALMON SALAD

Fish and watercress has long been one of those magic flavour combinations. In this recipe, we use that magic to full effect, bringing these two superfoods together with a few other nutrient-packed ingredients for maximum healthiness and taste.

Serves 1 as a main

1 fresh salmon fillet

½ ripe avocado

3 handfuls watercress

handful toasted pumpkin seeds

small handful goji berries

lemon wedges, to garnish

For the lemon dressing

2 tsp lemon juice

1 tbsp extra virgin olive oil

½ tsp Dijon mustard

unrefined salt and freshly
    ground black pepper

Preheat the oven to 180°C/350°F/Gas Mark 4.

Wrap the salmon fillet in foil, place on a baking tray (baking pan) and bake in the oven for 20 minutes. Unwrap the salmon and allow to cool. Flake into small bite-size pieces, discarding the skin.

Meanwhile, mix all the dressing ingredients together thoroughly in a bowl, adding salt and pepper to taste. Set aside.

Remove the avocado flesh from its skin with a teaspoon and toss with the watercress and dressing. Top with the salmon flakes, toasted pumpkin seeds and goji berries. Garnish with a few lemon wedges and serve.

WARM NEW POTATO & SMOKED MACKEREL SALAD

This deliciously filling main meal salad is a lovely lunch to share with friends. I have used spinach and rocket (arugula) here, but any baby leaf salad would work. Use a mayonnaise without additives, or try making your own.

Serves 2

200 g/7 oz new potatoes

salt

2 handfuls rocket (arugula) leaves

3 handfuls baby spinach leaves

1 large smoked mackerel fillet

For the mustard mayonnaise dressing

3 tbsp mayonnaise

zest and juice of ½ lemon

1 tsp Dijon mustard

unrefined salt and freshly ground black pepper

Bring the new potatoes to the boil in plenty of salted water. Reduce the heat and simmer for 10–15 minutes until the point of a knife pushes easily into the centre of a potato without breaking it apart. Drain the potatoes and allow to cool while you make the dressing.

Mix all the dressing ingredients together thoroughly in a bowl, adding salt and pepper to taste. Set aside.

Once the potatoes are cool enough to handle, cut them in half. Toss them in the dressing and set aside.

Mix the rocket (arugula) and baby spinach leaves and put them in a salad bowl or onto two plates. Add the dressed potatoes. Remove the skin and break up the smoked mackerel fillet, placing it on top of the salad before serving.

TUNISIAN SARDINE SALAD

An exotic taste sensation, this salad is a sophisticated addition to any table. I like to use Niçoise olives here, but any type will work. Cook your own fresh sardines, if you prefer.

Serves 2

4 small potatoes, peeled

unrefined salt and freshly ground black pepper

handful mangetout (snow peas)

125 g/4 oz can sardines in olive oil

2 large heirloom or vine tomatoes, sliced

5 cherry tomatoes, halved

¼ cucumber, finely sliced

handful good-quality olives

1 small fennel bulb, finely sliced

1 small red onion, peeled and finely sliced

1 red chili, finely sliced

small handful toasted almonds, finely sliced

olive oil, for drizzling

Cook the potatoes in plenty of salted water until firm but cooked through, about 15–20 minutes. Drain and allow to cool until they are easy to handle. Slice into 5 mm/¼ inch thick rounds.

Blanch the mangetout (snow peas) by putting them in a bowl and soaking them in boiling water for 10 minutes. Drain before using.

Break up the sardines into large pieces. Gently toss all the salad ingredients together. Drizzle with olive oil, adding salt and pepper to taste.

FENNEL & MIZUNA SALAD
with Dried Mulberries

Mizuna leaves, also known as Japanese mustard greens, are not always easy to find, but are well worth the effort of searching them out (or growing your own). Their spicy flavour works beautifully with subtly sweet dried mulberries and aromatic fennel. If you can't find mizuna, try substituting with (rocket) arugula or young mustard greens.

Serves 2 as a side

2 handfuls mixed mizuna leaves
½ fennel bulb, very finely sliced
handful dried mulberries

For the simple dressing

3 tbsp extra virgin olive oil
1 tsp cider vinegar
unrefined salt and freshly ground black pepper

Mix all the dressing ingredients together thoroughly in a bowl, adding salt and pepper to taste. Set aside.

Lay a bed of mizuna leaves prettily on a serving plate, or two side plates. Pile the fennel in the centre and scatter over the dried mulberries. Finish with a drizzle of dressing.

SUPER-BERRY SALAD

Summer is the time to make the most of superfood berries. Their subtle sweetness and flavour lend themselves beautifully to leafy salads. Try using this raspberry dressing with other salad recipes for a fruity twist.

Serves 4 as a side

1 soft round lettuce, shredded

handful basil leaves

handful fresh raspberries

handful stoned (pitted) fresh cherries

handful blueberries

½ small red onion, peeled and finely sliced

For the raspberry dressing

1 tbsp extra virgin olive oil

1 tbsp raspberry or cider vinegar

2 handfuls fresh raspberries

unrefined salt and freshly ground black pepper

Using a hand blender, or jug blender, blend all the dressing ingredients together, adding salt and pepper to taste. Set aside.

On a large plate or in a salad bowl, toss the shredded lettuce and basil.

Sprinkle over the fresh berries and onion and drizzle with the dressing just before serving.

FARRO BUDDHA BOWL

Farro is traditionally used in Italian cooking, so you will find it in Italian delicatessens, upmarket supermarkets, grocery stores and online. Take note that this deliciously nutty grain does not expand as much as rice or quinoa once it is cooked.

Serves 2

500 ml/18 fl oz/2 cups vegetable stock

200 g/7 oz/1 cup farro, well rinsed

1 medium sweet potato, diced

extra virgin olive oil, for drizzling

unrefined salt and freshly ground black pepper

100 g/3½ oz/¾ cup canned sweetcorn, drained

¼ cucumber, diced

200 g/7 oz/1½ cups canned chickpeas, rinsed

2 small handfuls blueberries

2 small handfuls cooked edamame beans

pea shoots or rocket (arugula) leaves, to garnish

Preheat the oven to 200°C/400°F/Gas Mark 6. Bring the stock to the boil in a pan, then add the farro. Bring back to the boil, reduce the heat and simmer for 30 minutes. Once cooked, drain any remaining liquid.

Place the sweet potato on a baking tray (baking pan) and toss with olive oil and salt and pepper to taste. Bake in the oven for 20 minutes until beginning to crisp. Halfway through baking, add the sweetcorn on a separate part of the baking tray.

Serve the farro in bowls, drizzled with olive oil. Top the farro with the sweet potato, sweetcorn and remaining ingredients. Serve warm.

FREEKEH SALAD
with Pomegranate Dressing

Pomegranate seeds are a gorgeous addition to any salad – their jewel-like brightness is a joy to behold. The syrup made from pomegranates is sweet and tart; it makes a wonderful marinade and is great in all kinds of salad dressings.

Serves 1 as a main or 3 as a side

100 g/3½ oz/½ cup freekeh

250 ml/8 fl oz/1 cup lightly salted water

½ red pepper, finely diced

2 handfuls toasted pumpkin seeds

1 tbsp very finely chopped mint leaves

3 handfuls pomegranate seeds

100 g/3½ oz feta cheese, crumbled

For the dressing

1 tbsp pomegranate syrup/molasses

3 tbsp extra virgin olive oil

1 garlic clove, peeled and crushed

unrefined salt and freshly ground
   black pepper

In a lidded saucepan, bring the freekeh to the boil in the lightly salted water. Reduce the heat, cover and simmer for 15–20 minutes. Remove from the heat and allow to cool, uncovered.

Meanwhile, mix all the ingredients for the dressing together thoroughly in a bowl, adding salt and pepper to taste. Set aside.

Toss the cooked freekeh with the red pepper, toasted pumpkin seeds, mint leaves and dressing.

Sprinkle over the pomegranate seeds and crumbled feta before serving.

SOUPS

BASIC BONE BROTH

'Bone broth' is essentially stock. However, you cook it for much longer than the average stock, so, as well as being a fantastic soup base, it is an amazingly nutrient-dense warming drink, filled with protein, gelatin and trace minerals. You can save chicken or beef bones from other meals, freezing them until you have enough to make this bone broth. Because you will be cooking this for many hours, cover the bones in plenty of water in the pan so that all the water doesn't evaporate.

1 kg/2 lb 4 oz organic chicken or beef bones
2 celery sticks, roughly chopped
1 onion, peeled and roughly chopped
handful parsley
2 bay leaves
2 tbsp cider vinegar
1 tbsp unrefined salt (optional)

Preheat the oven to 200°C/400°F/Gas Mark 6. Place the bones, celery and onion in a roasting pan and roast for 30 minutes, or until beginning to brown.

Place the roasted bones and vegetables in a stockpot. Add the parsley, bay leaves, vinegar and salt, if using. Cover generously with water and bring to the boil. Reduce the heat to a low simmer and cook for at least 6 hours, or overnight.

Strain the broth and leave to stand until cooled. Store in the refrigerator for up to 5 days or freeze in batches.

Note

Bone broth becomes gelatinous when cold.

PUMPKIN & GINGER SOUP

This is such a pretty soup. It works equally well as a dinner party starter (appetizer) or a relaxed lunch. The best croutons are homemade – simply shallow-fry cubes of bread in olive oil and season with salt and freshly ground black pepper.

Serves 2

250 g/9 oz pumpkin, peeled, seeded and diced

1 medium carrot, peeled and chopped

1 tbsp very finely chopped ginger

1 garlic clove, peeled and very finely chopped

1 tsp ground coriander

½ tsp ground turmeric

200 ml/7 fl oz/¾ cup canned coconut milk

400 ml/14 fl oz/1⅔ cups vegetable stock or
   bone broth (*see* page 122)

unrefined salt

To garnish (optional)

rosemary leaves

finely chopped chives

croutons

pomegranate syrup/molasses
   (optional)

For the soup, place the pumpkin, carrot, ginger, garlic, coriander, turmeric, coconut milk and stock or broth in a medium saucepan. Bring to the boil, reduce the heat to a simmer and cook with the lid on for 30 minutes.

Blend the soup until smooth, adding salt to taste, if necessary.

To garnish, divide the soup between two bowls and sprinkle over a few rosemary leaves, chives and croutons. Add a small amount of pomegranate syrup if you have it.

KALE SOUP
with Pistachio Seed Sprinkle

There is nothing quite like a green soup to make you feel like you are eating healthily. You can serve this recipe without the seed sprinkle, but if you want a sophisticated flourish, don't miss it out.

Serves 2

2 tbsp extra virgin olive oil

1 large leek (about 250 g/9 oz), chopped

2 garlic cloves, peeled and very finely chopped

100 g/3½ oz curly kale, tough stems removed

small bunch parsley

500 ml/18 fl oz/2 cups vegetable stock or
   bone broth (*see* page 122)

100 ml/3½ fl oz/⅓ cup unsweetened oat milk

unrefined salt and freshly ground black pepper

oat cream, to serve (optional)

For the pistachio seed sprinkle

1 tsp coriander seeds

1 tbsp sesame seeds

1 tbsp sunflower seeds

3 tbsp shelled roasted pistachios

1 tbsp flaxseeds

pinch unrefined salt

a few grinds black pepper

Heat the olive oil in a lidded saucepan over a medium heat. Add the leek and sauté for 10 minutes until soft. Stir in the garlic and cook for a further 2 minutes.

Add the rest of the soup ingredients. Bring to the boil, reduce the heat, cover and simmer for 15 minutes. Once cooked, blend until smooth, adding salt and pepper to taste, if necessary.

To make the sprinkle, toast the coriander seeds, sesame seeds and sunflower seeds in a dry frying pan over a medium heat for a few minutes, shaking the pan to toast evenly. Once the seeds begin to brown, remove from the heat and allow to cool.

Grind all the sprinkle ingredients together in a spice grinder or in a mortar with a pestle until it is a coarse powder.

Serve the soup hot in bowls, drizzle over a little oat cream and top with the pistachio seed sprinkle.

AUTUMN DETOX BEETROOT SOUP

Beetroot (beet) is one of my favourite vegetables to cook with. Not only is it packed full of goodness, the colour makes my mouth water before I've taken a mouthful. The hues in this soup are simply gorgeous!

Serves 4

2 tbsp olive oil

1 medium red onion, peeled and roughly chopped

1 garlic clove, peeled and very finely chopped

1 tbsp very finely chopped ginger

1 tsp toasted cumin seeds

3 medium beetroot (beets), roughly chopped

2 celery sticks, roughly chopped

1 medium carrot, peeled and roughly chopped

½ cooking apple, peeled, cored and roughly chopped

750 ml/1¼ pints/3¼ cups vegetable stock or bone broth (*see* page 122)

½ tsp unrefined salt

freshly ground black pepper

For the topping

1 tbsp shelled pistachios, lightly chopped

1 tbsp pumpkin seeds

1 tbsp flaxseeds

1 tbsp chia seeds

4 dessert spoons live yogurt

about 20 mint leaves

Heat the olive oil in a medium lidded saucepan and sauté the onion over a low heat until the onion is transparent. Add the garlic, ginger and toasted cumin seeds and cook for a few minutes. Next, add the vegetables, apple and stock or broth. Bring to the boil, reduce the heat, cover and simmer for 40 minutes.

Meanwhile, prepare the topping. Mix the pistachios with the pumpkin seeds, flaxseeds and chia seeds in a bowl.

Once the soup is cooked, blend until smooth, adding salt and pepper to taste, if necessary.

To serve, pour the soup into bowls. Lightly stir a spoonful of yogurt into the centre of each bowl, and sprinkle all the seeds and mint leaves on top.

CAULIFLOWER CURRY SOUP
with Coconut Milk

You might think that cauliflower is an unusual choice for soup. Combined here with coconut milk, it takes on a subtle loveliness that soothes the soul – true comfort food on a grey day.

Serves 3

2 tbsp extra virgin coconut oil

1 medium onion, peeled and diced

2 garlic cloves, peeled and very finely chopped

500 g/1 lb 2 oz cauliflower florets

400 ml/14 fl oz/1⅔ cups coconut milk

400 ml/14 fl oz/1⅔ cups vegetable stock or
    bone broth (*see* page 122)

1 tsp ground coriander

½ tsp ground cumin

1 tsp paprika

unrefined salt (optional)

To garnish

coconut milk

paprika

cold-pressed flaxseed oil (optional)

coriander (cilantro) leaves

Heat the coconut oil in a medium lidded saucepan and sauté the onion for 10 minutes until translucent. Next, add the garlic and cook for a further 2 minutes. Finally, add the rest of the soup ingredients and bring to the boil. Reduce the heat, cover and simmer for 20 minutes.

Once the soup is cooked, blend until smooth and creamy. If necessary, add salt to taste.

Serve in warmed bowls and top with a little coconut milk, paprika, flaxseed oil and coriander (cilantro) leaves.

RICH TOMATO SOUP

This recipe is inspired by classic canned tomato soup. It is all the more delicious because of the freshness and depth of flavour that happens when you make it at home with top-quality ingredients.

Serves 2

3 tbsp olive oil

1 medium red onion, peeled and chopped

1 garlic clove, peeled and very finely chopped

400 g/14 oz can organic chopped tomatoes

200 ml/7 fl oz/¾ cup vegetable stock or bone broth (*see* page 122)

1 tbsp fresh thyme leaves

½ tsp maple syrup or honey

1 tbsp lemon juice

¼ tsp unrefined salt

freshly ground black pepper

Heat the olive oil in a medium saucepan and sauté the onion for 10 minutes until translucent. Stir in the garlic and cook for 2 minutes. Add all the remaining ingredients. Bring to the boil, then reduce the heat and simmer, uncovered, for 15 minutes.

Blend until totally smooth, then serve with healthy bread or a gluten-free bread-alternative.

HEARTY LENTIL SOUP

There is nothing quite like a hearty lentil soup to warm your bones on a cold day. I have added bacon here, but to make the recipe vegan, just leave it out and use vegetable stock.

Serves 2

1 small onion, peeled and finely diced

2 bacon rashers (slices), finely diced (optional)

1 tbsp olive oil

1 garlic clove, peeled and very finely chopped

½ yellow pepper, finely diced

1 small carrot, peeled and finely diced

1 tsp ground coriander

½ tsp ground cumin

½ tsp ground cinnamon

100 g/3½ oz/½ cup green lentils, rinsed

500 ml/18 fl oz/2 cups vegetable stock or bone broth (*see* page 122), unsalted, if
    using bacon

coriander (cilantro) leaves, to garnish

In a saucepan, sauté the onion and bacon, if using, in the olive oil until the onion is translucent. Stir in the garlic, yellow pepper, carrot and spices and cook for a further 5 minutes. Add the lentils and stock or broth. Bring to the boil, then reduce the heat and simmer for 30–40 minutes until the lentils are beginning to split open.

Serve with a sprinkling of coriander (cilantro) leaves on top.

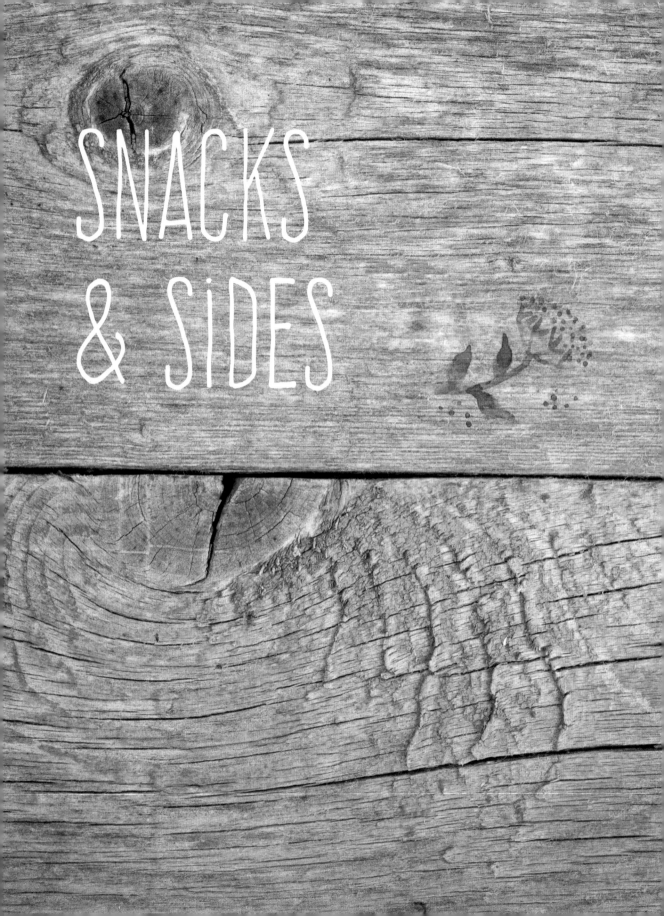

SNACKS
& SIDES

CLASSIC KIMCHI

Traditionally, this recipe calls for a fish flavouring, but to make vegan kimchi, simply replace the fish sauce with water. Chlorinated tap water inhibits the fermentation process, so use spring or filtered water.

1 medium head Chinese (napa) cabbage (about 1 kg/2 lb 4 oz)

125 g/4 oz/½ cup unrefined salt

enough filtered or spring water to cover the cabbage

1 tbsp grated garlic

1 tbsp grated fresh ginger

1 tsp date syrup

3 tbsp fish sauce or water

1–5 tbsp Korean red pepper flakes (gochugaru)

225 g/8 oz mooli (daikon radish), peeled and cut into matchsticks

Cut the cabbage into quarters along its length. Cut out the cores and discard. Cut across each quarter to make 2.5 cm/1 inch chunks. Put the cabbage into a large bowl with the salt, massaging with your hands until the cabbage starts to wilt and soften. Pour enough water over to cover the cabbage. Keep the cabbage submerged by putting a plate on top of it, with something heavy on top of the plate, such as a jar or can, and leave to stand for 2 hours.

To make the kimchi paste, in a small bowl, mix the garlic, ginger, date syrup and fish sauce or water into a paste, adding the Korean red pepper flakes to your preferred spiciness.

Drain the cabbage in a colander and rinse thoroughly under cold running water. Leave to drain for 20 minutes. With your hands or the back of a large spoon, squeeze any remaining water from the cabbage.

Thoroughly stir the cabbage, kimchi paste and mooli (daikon) together in a mixing bowl until the paste is evenly distributed. Pack the kimchi into sterilized jars (you can sterilize jars by placing them in a medium oven for 10 minutes and allowing to cool), pressing down firmly until the juices rise to cover the vegetables. Leave at least 2.5 cm/1 inch of space at the top of each jar and seal the jars with the lids.

Leave the jars to stand on a plate (just in case of seepage) at room temperature for 1–5 days. Each day, open the jars and press the cabbage down to keep it submerged. Taste each day, and refrigerate when the taste is right for you. Eat it at this point or leave for another week or two in the refrigerator for the flavours to develop.

MUNG BEAN FRITTATAS
with Hemp Seeds

These superfood mini frittatas are quick and easy to make. Serve them as a superfood snack, or as part of a light lunch alongside your choice of salad from the Salads chapter (pages 98–119).

Makes 4

unrefined salt and freshly ground black pepper

100 g/3½ oz/1¼ cups grated courgette (zucchini)

1 egg

1 tbsp cornflour (cornstarch)

1 garlic clove, peeled and crushed

2 tbsp grated Parmesan cheese or 1 tbsp nutritional yeast

½ tsp Dijon mustard

100 g/3½ oz/¾ cup sprouted mung beans, finely chopped

3 tbsp hulled hemp seeds

2 tbsp olive oil

Stir a little salt through the grated courgette (zucchini) and leave to stand for 20 minutes. Drain in a sieve (strainer), pushing it down with your hand or a spoon to squeeze out excess water.

Whisk together the egg with the cornflour (cornstarch), garlic, Parmesan or nutritional yeast, and mustard. Stir the mung bean sprouts into the egg mix with the hemp seeds. Add salt and pepper to taste.

Heat the olive oil in a nonstick frying pan over a medium heat. For each mini frittata, dollop 2–3 dessert spoonsful of the mixture into the pan and shape into a round with the back of the spoon. Cook over a medium-high heat for 2–3 minutes until the frittatas set and are lightly browned underneath. Flip over and cook for a further 2–3 minutes, again until lightly browned.

ROAST GARLIC & CAULIFLOWER MASH

If you are looking for a low-carb alternative to mashed potato, you have found the answer right here; cauliflower provides the comfort factor without the calories or sugar spike, and garlic may help to balance your blood sugar, too.

Serves 4 as a side

1 garlic bulb

2 tbsp olive oil

1 medium cauliflower, leaves removed, and broken into florets

2 tbsp butter or olive oil

unrefined salt

coriander (cilantro) leaves, to garnish (optional)

Preheat the oven to 220°C/425°F/Gas Mark 7.

To roast the garlic, leave the garlic bulb whole and slice the top off the bulb to expose a little of the cloves inside. Lay the bulb on a piece of foil and pour the olive oil over the garlic. Wrap up the bulb in the foil and bake in the oven for 35 minutes until soft. Allow to cool, then peel the garlic cloves.

Steam the cauliflower for 15 minutes until tender. Place the cooked cauliflower, butter or olive oil and the garlic cloves in a food processor or blender and process until smooth. Add salt to taste and garnish with a few coriander (cilantro) leaves before serving.

AÏOLI

Aïoli is a classic sauce eaten in southern France and northern Spain. It is delicious with a wide range of dishes, from sweet potato wedges to burgers, and can be used wherever you might use mayonnaise.

Makes roughly a 450 g/1 lb (16 oz) jar

1 large free-range egg yolk
1 tsp wholegrain mustard
250 ml/8 fl oz/1 cup light olive oil
2 tbsp lemon juice
3 tbsp water
1 garlic clove, peeled and crushed
unrefined salt and freshly ground black pepper

Whisk the egg yolk and mustard together in a bowl.

One tablespoon at a time, gently and thoroughly whisk in 5 tablespoons of the olive oil. Then start whisking in the oil in larger quantities. As the mixture thickens, whisk in the lemon juice. When all the oil is mixed in, thoroughly whisk in the water and stir in the garlic and salt and pepper to taste.

Chill in the refrigerator and eat within 5 days.

WALNUT, MUSHROOM & LENTIL PÂTÉ

This richly satisfying pâté is the perfect addition to a canapé selection, or on toast for breakfast. Add it to sandwiches with slices of juicy tomato and watercress for a nutrient-packed work lunch.

Makes roughly a 350 g/12 oz jar

50 g/2 oz/¼ cup uncooked brown lentils or 150 g/5 oz/1 cup cooked brown lentils

75 g/3 oz/¾ cup walnuts

3 tbsp olive oil

½ small white onion, peeled and diced

100 g/3½ oz chestnut (cremini) mushrooms

1 garlic clove, peeled and very finely chopped

2 tbsp water

1 tbsp lemon juice

½ tsp unrefined salt

chopped walnuts, to garnish

If cooking the lentils, bring them to the boil in a pan of plenty of water. Reduce the heat, cover and simmer for 30 minutes until soft. Drain when cooked.

Toast the nuts in a dry frying pan over a medium-low heat until lightly browned. Leave to cool.

Heat the olive oil in the frying pan and sauté the onion for 5–10 minutes until transparent. Add the mushrooms and garlic and cook for a further 5 minutes.

Blitz the cooked lentils, toasted walnuts, cooked onion, garlic and mushrooms with the water, lemon juice and salt in a mini food processor or blender until smooth and creamy. Serve topped with chopped walnuts.

SUPER SUMMER ROLLS

Summer rolls are perfect for those sunny days when all you want is something light and fresh. This recipe is great for parties and impressing friends too. Find your rice wrappers in Asian supermarkets or online.

Makes 16

1 firm ripe avocado, peeled, pitted
    and finely sliced
handful broccoli or alfalfa sprouts
1 medium carrot, peeled and julienned
2 handfuls baby salad leaves
handful fresh parsley sprigs
1 tbsp chia seeds (optional)
16 small rice paper wrappers

For the dipping sauce

4 tbsp date syrup
2 tbsp gluten-free tamari
2 tbsp water
1 tsp red chili (pepper) flakes
2 garlic cloves, peeled and crushed
2 tsp grated ginger
5 cm/2 in piece cucumber, finely diced
3 tbsp toasted chopped peanuts

For the dipping sauce, stir the date syrup, tamari and water together. Add the rest of the ingredients and mix thoroughly. Allow the flavours to meld while you make the rolls.

For the summer rolls, have all your filling ingredients prepared in advance. To soften the rice paper wrappers, fill a large bowl with hot water – not too hot, but hot enough to soften the wrappers. Make one summer roll at a time.

Dip a wrapper in the water until just soft enough to be pliable. Lay the softened wrapper on a flat surface. Leaving a 2.5 cm/1 inch space at the bottom of the wrapper, lay your fillings in the middle so that they stick over the edge (when you wrap a roll, a little of the filling will stick prettily out of the top). Fold the bottom of the wrapper up, and wrap the sides over to create a roll. Sprinkle over some chia seeds, if using, and put on a serving dish, fold-side down. Continue until all your rolls are made. Serve with the dipping sauce.

KALE TAPENADE WITH SPIRULINA

Tapenade is traditionally made with anchovies. This vegan version employs the sea taste of spirulina instead, making this a super-charged green sauce that works equally well as a dip or with vegan burgers.

Makes roughly a 175 g/6 oz jar

50 g/2 oz kale, stems removed, and roughly chopped

25 g/1 oz/¼ cup good-quality pitted green olives

3 tbsp pumpkin seeds

2 tbsp olive oil

¼ tsp spirulina

3 tbsp capers

1 garlic clove, peeled and crushed

handful basil leaves

1 tbsp lemon juice

Blitz all the ingredients into a rough paste in a mini food processor.

Serve with burgers, frittatas, fish and meat for a deliciously nutritious super-food hit. Chill in the refrigerator for up to 5 days.

BRAZIL NUT HUMMUS

This rich and creamy hummus variation is packed full of nutrients and will keep you feeling full and satisfied for hours. Use it as a dip, as a spread on toast or as a filling for sandwiches.

Makes roughly a 350 g/12 oz jar

150 g/5 oz/1¼ cups Brazil nuts, roughly chopped
1 small garlic clove, peeled and crushed
juice of 1 lemon
½ tsp unrefined salt
3 tbsp olive oil
3 tbsp water

Blitz all the ingredients together in a blender or mini food processor until smooth and creamy.

Chill in the refrigerator for up to 4 days.

MAINS

QUINOA RISOTTO WITH PUMPKIN

Risotto is traditionally made with rice. This quinoa version is much quicker and less labour intensive – delicious comfort food for a cold day. If pumpkins are not in season, substitute butternut squash, usually available all year around.

Serves 2

1 tbsp olive oil

½ small onion, peeled and finely diced

1 garlic clove, peeled and crushed

100 g/3½ oz pumpkin, peeled and grated

150 g/5 oz/¾ cup quinoa

250 ml/8 fl oz/1 cup vegetable or chicken stock

50 g/2 oz Parmesan cheese, shaved

4 sage leaves, finely sliced

Heat the olive oil in a saucepan, add the onion and sauté until transparent. Add the garlic and grated pumpkin and cook for a further 5 minutes, stirring regularly.

Add the quinoa and 1 large ladle of stock. Bring to the boil, then reduce the heat and simmer. Keep adding stock until the quinoa is cooked through, stirring constantly for 10 minutes.

Once cooked, divide between two serving dishes. Top with shaved Parmesan and sliced sage leaves.

BEET & QUINOA BURGERS

These beautiful burgers will brighten up your day. For extra pizzazz, make them up with the turmeric burger buns on page 183, the aïoli on page 146 and the kale tapenade on page 155. Who knew burgers could be so good for you?

Makes 4

For the burgers

165 g/5½ oz/1 cup quinoa

400 ml/14 fl oz/1⅔ cups water

1 vegan or vegetarian stock cube

325 g/11½ oz cooked beetroot (beet)

2 tbsp olive oil

1 tsp toasted cumin seeds

2 tsp toasted coriander seeds

1 tbsp lemon juice

2 garlic cloves, peeled and crushed

unrefined salt and freshly ground black pepper

To assemble

2 tbsp olive oil

4 burger buns, halved
   and toasted

baby salad leaves

1 ripe avocado, peeled, pitted and sliced

1 large tomato, sliced

½ red onion, peeled and sliced into rings

Preheat the oven to 180°C/350°F/Gas Mark 4. Bring the quinoa, water and stock cube to the boil in a pan, then reduce the heat and simmer for 10 minutes.

Meanwhile, blend the cooked beetroot (beet) with the olive oil, spices, lemon juice and garlic into a purée. Stir into the cooked quinoa and add salt and pepper to taste. Shape the mixture into burgers, place on a baking tray lined with baking parchment and bake in the oven for 25 minutes.

To assemble the burgers, spread olive oil on the insides of the buns, then layer the remaining ingredients between the burger halves.

VEGGIE BUCKWHEAT NOODLES

Mirin is a type of Asian cooking wine. Its unique flavour gives stir-fries a delicious twist. Have all your ingredients ready, as once you start cooking, you will need to move fast.

Serves 2

150 g/5 oz buckwheat noodles

1 tbsp sesame seeds

2 tbsp extra virgin coconut oil

1 tbsp very finely chopped ginger

4 garlic cloves, peeled and very finely chopped

50 g/2 oz/½ cup finely sliced red cabbage

1 medium carrot, peeled and cut into matchsticks

2 spring onions (scallions), sliced

2 tbsp tamari

2 tsp mirin (optional)

coriander (cilantro) leaves, to garnish

Cook the buckwheat noodles until *al dente*, following the packet instructions. Quickly drain and rinse under cold running water to stop them cooking.

Toast the sesame seeds in a dry pan over a medium heat, shaking the pan constantly, until lightly browned.

Melt the coconut oil in a wok or large frying pan over a high heat. Add the ginger and garlic and fry for 30 seconds. Add the cabbage and carrot and cook for about 4 minutes, stirring until beginning to soften. Add the noodles and gently stir until heated through. Finally, add the spring onions (scallions), tamari, mirin, if using, and sesame seeds and stir through. Remove from the heat and serve immediately topped with coriander (cilantro) leaves.

SALMON & BROCCOLI TAGLIATELLE

I have used spelt pasta here, since spelt is an ancient strain of wheat that contains more nutrients and less gluten than modern strains. Or, of course, you can use your favourite gluten-free pasta. I think that tagliatelle works particularly well with this dish, but you could easily substitute penne.

Serves 2

250 g/9 oz fresh salmon fillets

150 g/5 oz broccoli florets

150 g/5 oz white spelt tagliatelle

125 g/4 oz/½ cup mild soft goat's cheese

2 tbsp water

2 garlic cloves, peeled and finely chopped

¼ tsp unrefined salt

olive oil, for tossing

1 tbsp capers

freshly ground black pepper

Preheat the oven to 180°C/350°F/Gas Mark 4. Wrap the salmon fillets in foil and bake in the oven for 20 minutes. When cooked, remove the skin and break into bite-size pieces.

Meanwhile, steam the broccoli for 10 minutes, then refresh under cold running water to stop it cooking.

Cook the tagliatelle following the packet instructions.

While the tagliatelle is cooking, melt the goat's cheese with the water in a pan over a medium-low heat. Stir in the garlic and salt, allowing the sauce to bubble gently for a few minutes. Gently stir through the salmon and broccoli and cook for a few minutes until warmed through.

Drain the tagliatelle and toss with a little olive oil. Divide the tagliatelle between two pasta bowls, topping with the salmon and broccoli sauce. Sprinkle over the capers and season with black pepper before serving.

WALNUT LOAF
with Mediterranean Brussels Sprouts

This is a wonderful nut loaf for special occasions or when catering for the vegetarian loved ones in your life. If you want to change someone's mind about Brussels sprouts, the accompaniment is a winner too.

Serves 6–8

3 tbsp olive oil, plus extra for oiling

200 g/7 oz spinach

1 medium onion, peeled and finely diced

10 sage leaves, very finely chopped

4 garlic cloves, peeled and crushed

300 g/11 oz/3 cups walnuts

200 g/7 oz/2¼ cups cooked chestnuts

1 thick slice white bread

½ tsp lemon juice

50 ml/2 fl oz/¼ cup vegetable stock

50 g/2 oz/½ cup dried cranberries (no added sugar)

200 g/7 oz/1 cup cream cheese or vegan cream cheese

¼ tsp unrefined salt

freshly ground black pepper

For the basil and olive Brussels sprouts

1 tbsp olive oil

2 garlic cloves, peeled and very finely chopped

500 g/1 lb 2 oz Brussels sprouts, trimmed and roughly sliced

100 g/3½ oz/¾ cup pitted black olives, halved

unrefined salt and freshly ground black pepper

Preheat the oven to 180°C/350°F/Gas Mark 4. Oil a 900 g/2 lb loaf tin (pan) with olive oil.

Steam the spinach for 5–10 minutes until cooked. Allow to cool, then squeeze out excess water from the spinach.

Heat the olive oil in a frying pan, add the onion and sage and sauté until the onion is transparent. Add the garlic and cook for a further 2 minutes.

In a food processor or by hand, chop the walnuts, chestnuts and bread into breadcrumb-size pieces. In a mixing bowl, combine the chopped walnut mix with the sautéed onion, sage and garlic plus the lemon juice, stock, cranberries, 100 g/3½ oz/½ cup of the cream cheese and salt and pepper to taste.

Spoon half of the walnut loaf mix into the loaf tin. Flatten and press down the mixture. Spread the remaining 100 g/3½ oz/½ cup cream cheese on top. Next, spread the spinach over evenly. Finally, add the remaining walnut loaf mix, flattening and pressing down to help the loaf stick together.

Bake in the oven for 35–40 minutes until lightly browned. Turn the loaf out of the tin to serve.

For the sprouts, heat the olive oil in a frying pan or wok, add the garlic and cook for 1 minute. Throw in the sliced sprouts and sauté over a medium-high heat for 6 minutes. Add the olives and salt and pepper to taste and cook for a further minute. Serve in a warmed serving dish with the loaf.

THAI YELLOW CURRY

Nothing beats homemade Thai curry paste but, if you want to save time, try sourcing a jarred version online – it is unusual to find it in shops. To make this dish vegan, replace the chicken with tofu.

Serves 4

For the Thai yellow curry paste

1 tbsp coconut oil

1 large shallot, peeled and quartered

8 whole garlic cloves, peeled

3 tbsp very finely chopped ginger

4 dried red bird's-eye (Thai) chilies

½ tsp unrefined salt

1 tbsp ground turmeric

1 tbsp curry powder

1 tsp roasted ground coriander

1 tbsp lemongrass paste

For the curry

2 tbsp extra virgin coconut oil

1 tsp mustard seeds

4 tbsp Thai yellow curry paste

1 medium onion, peeled and diced

2 chicken breasts, cubed,
    or 200 g/7 oz tofu, cubed

2 small potatoes, peeled and cubed

1 orange pepper, diced

400 ml/14 fl oz/1⅔ cups coconut milk

20 mangetout (snow peas)

To garnish

1 mild red chili, finely sliced
basil leaves

To make the curry paste, heat the coconut oil in a small pan over a medium-low heat. Add the shallot, whole garlic cloves and ginger and cook for about 7 minutes until the shallots are translucent and the garlic is slightly browned. Blitz all the paste ingredients in a mini food processor, adding water 1 tablespoon at a time to help it turn, if necessary. Alternatively, mash to a paste in a mortar with a pestle.

To make the curry, heat the coconut oil in a medium pan over a medium-high heat. Add the mustard seeds and cook, covered with a lid, until the seeds pop. Add the curry paste, onion and chicken or tofu and fry for 5 minutes, stirring regularly. Next, add the potatoes, orange pepper and coconut milk. Bring to the boil, reduce the heat, cover and simmer for 30 minutes. Five minutes before the end of the cooking time, stir through the mangetout (snow peas).

Serve with rice and garnish with the chili and basil leaves.

SEAWEED TAGLIATELLE
with Tomato Chipotle Sauce

Seaweed is unbelievably good for you and if you are trying to cut back on carbs, it is a delicious high-protein alternative. Find sea spaghetti in good health food stores or online.

Serves 2

3 tbsp olive oil

1 small red onion, peeled and sliced

2 garlic cloves, peeled and crushed

6 vine tomatoes, quartered

1 tsp lemon juice

1 tsp maple syrup

1 cinnamon stick

1 smoked chipotle chili, plus extra to garnish (optional)

unrefined salt and freshly ground black pepper

40 g/1½ oz sea spaghetti

Heat 2 tbsp olive oil in a saucepan, add the sliced onion and sauté for about 10 minutes until transparent. Add the garlic and cook for a further 2 minutes.

Add the tomatoes to the pan with the lemon juice, maple syrup, cinnamon stick and chipotle chili. Bring to the boil, then reduce the heat, cover and simmer for 20 minutes, stirring occasionally. Add salt and pepper to taste.

Bring another pan of water to the boil and add the sea spaghetti. Cook for 10 minutes until supple. To serve, toss the sea spaghetti in the remaining olive oil and a little salt. Divide between two pasta bowls, topping the sea spaghetti with the sauce. Garnish with extra slices of chipotle chili, if you wish.

CHEESY-KALE-&-OAT-CRUST PIZZA

The flavoursome crust of this pizza is a lovely alternative to the traditional wheat pizza base. It also makes great sandwiches, in place of the bread. Try it with all your favourite pizza toppings and fillings.

Makes 1 medium pizza

For the pizza base

100 g/3½ oz kale, stems removed

2 tbsp olive oil

50 ml/2 fl oz/¼ cup water

2 crushed garlic cloves

75 g/3 oz/¾ cup jumbo oats

150 g/5 oz/1⅔ cups grated organic Cheddar cheese

unrefined salt and freshly ground black pepper

For the topping

2 chestnut (cremini) mushrooms, sliced

1 red onion, peeled and sliced

3 cherry tomatoes, sliced

Preheat the oven to 180°C/350°F/Gas Mark 4. Line a baking sheet with baking parchment.

For the base, steam the kale for 10 minutes, then blitz in a food processor or chop finely by hand.

In a mixing bowl, combine all the base ingredients, adding salt and pepper to taste. Spread the pizza base mix out on the baking sheet, into a circle about 1 cm/½ inch deep. Bake for 10 minutes until the cheese begins to melt. Remove from the oven and increase the oven temperature to 200°C/400°F/Gas Mark 6.

Distribute your topping ingredients over the pizza base and return to the oven for a further 10–15 minutes before serving.

BREADS & BAKES

OAT-CRUST SQUASH & ONION TART

Squashes are so beautiful, and wonderful to cook with. In this recipe, I have used yellow summer squash, but feel free to use whichever seasonal variety is available in your local veg shop.

Serves 4–6

For the crust

butter or olive oil, for greasing

125 g/4 oz/¾ cup rolled oats

3 tbsp coarsely ground brown or golden flaxseeds

pinch unrefined salt

½ tsp bicarbonate of soda (baking soda)

40 g/1½ oz/3 tbsp cold cubed butter or dairy-free margarine

2 tsp cider vinegar

1 tbsp water

For the filling

400 g/14 oz/1⅔ cups hummus

1 small red onion, peeled, halved and thinly sliced

75 g/3 oz yellow summer squash, thinly sliced

unrefined salt and freshly ground black pepper

olive oil, for brushing

basil leaves, finely chopped

Preheat the oven to 180°C/350°F/Gas Mark 4. Grease an 18 cm/7 inch fluted pie tin (pan) with butter or olive oil.

In a blender jug or spice grinder, blitz the rolled oats into a flour.

Combine the oat flour, flaxseeds, salt and bicarbonate of soda (baking soda) in a large bowl. Using your fingertips, rub in the butter or margarine until there are no lumps of butter or margarine left. Knead in the vinegar and water to bind the dough together.

With wet fingertips, press the pastry into the bottom and up the sides of the pie tin. Bake the crust for 10 minutes.

Remove the crust from the oven and fill evenly with the hummus.

Alternating the red onion and the squash, layer the vegetables prettily over the top of the pie. Sprinkle over a little salt and black pepper. Brush with olive oil and bake in the oven for 35–45 minutes until the vegetables are cooked and soft.

Add the basil just before serving.

TURMERIC BURGER BUNS

The amazing bright yellow of these buns comes from the turmeric, said to be one of the most healing spices known to man. These beautiful rolls are sure to impress friends and family and are wonderful with soup as well as burgers.

Makes 6 buns

250 g/9 oz/1¾ cups white spelt flour, plus extra for dusting

2 tsp ground turmeric

½ tsp unrefined salt

2¼ tsp easy-blend dried yeast (active dry yeast)

175 ml/6 fl oz/scant ¾ cup unsweetened dairy-free milk (e.g. hemp milk), plus
    extra for glazing

2 tbsp extra virgin olive oil

1 tbsp honey or maple syrup

1 tsp chia seeds

Line a large baking sheet with baking parchment.

Sift the flour, turmeric and salt into a large mixing bowl, add the yeast and thoroughly mix together.

In a small saucepan, gently heat the milk, olive oil and honey or maple syrup until warm to the touch (do not overheat, as it will kill the yeast when it comes into contact with it).

Mix the dry and wet ingredients together to make a soft dough, adding a little flour if it is sticky.

Turn out onto a floured work surface and knead for 2 minutes until soft and elastic. Flour the bottom of the mixing bowl and put the dough back in the bowl. Cover and leave to stand for 10 minutes.

After 10 minutes, gently shape the dough into a sausage shape. Cut the dough in half, then each half into thirds to make 6 rolls. Briefly knead each roll into a round and place on the baking sheet, leaving plenty of space between each roll. Cover and put in a warm place to rise until doubled in size, about 45–60 minutes.

Preheat the oven to 160°C/325°F/Gas Mark 3.

Brush with a little milk and sprinkle with chia seeds, then bake in the oven for 15 minutes until fluffy and yellow. Serve warm or cold.

QUINOA & CHIA BREAD

This is a true superfood loaf. Gluten-free, dairy-free and sugar-free, it can be used as part of a Paleo diet. It is not as robust as gluten breads, so be gentle when slicing so that it retains its shape.

Makes 1 loaf

250 g/9 oz/1½ cups white quinoa, rinsed
5 tbsp chia seeds
750 ml/1¼ pints/3¼ cups water
olive oil or coconut oil, for greasing
2 tbsp sunflower seeds

Mix the quinoa, chia seeds and water together in a bowl. Leave to stand for 2 hours, or overnight, until the water is absorbed and the mixture is gelatinous. Stir thoroughly to evenly combine the quinoa and chia seeds.

Preheat the oven to 180°C/350°F/Gas Mark 4 and grease a 1 lb/900 g loaf tin (pan) with olive or coconut oil.

Spoon the bread mixture into the loaf tin, then sprinkle with sunflower seeds, pressing down lightly to help them stick.

Bake in the oven for 50–60 minutes until lightly golden in colour. Remove from the tin and leave to cool on a wire rack.

Store in the refrigerator and eat within 4 days. Alternatively, cut into slices and freeze.

GLUTEN-FREE BUCKWHEAT LOAF

Buckwheat has been used as a staple grain in France for years – traditionally used to make galettes (French-style pancakes). It works beautifully in this loaf, giving it a nutty flavour that is delicious toasted for breakfast and with soups.

Makes 1 loaf

olive oil, for greasing

200 g/7 oz/1½ cups gluten-free brown bread flour

300 g/11 oz/2½ cups buckwheat flour, plus extra for dusting

2 tsp easy-blend dried yeast (active dry yeast)

1 tsp unrefined salt

50 g/2 oz/⅓ cup sunflower seeds

3 tbsp flaxseeds

400 ml/14 fl oz/1⅔ cups unsweetened dairy-free milk (e.g. oat milk)

6 tbsp extra virgin olive oil

1 tsp cider vinegar

1 egg white or 20 g/¾ oz/2 tbsp chickpea flour, plus 4 tbsp water

1 tbsp honey or maple syrup

Grease a 900 g/2 lb loaf (pan) with olive oil. Sift the flours, yeast and salt into a large bowl, then mix in the seeds.

In a separate bowl or a jug, whisk the dairy-free milk, olive oil, vinegar, egg white or chickpea flour and water and honey or maple syrup together.

Stir together the dry and wet ingredients thoroughly to form a sticky dough. Spread evenly into the loaf tin. Cover with oiled plastic wrap and leave to stand in a warm place until the dough reaches the top of the tin, about 45–60 minutes.

Preheat the oven to 180°C/350°F/Gas Mark 4.

With an oiled knife, score a line along the length of the top of the loaf. Dust the top with buckwheat flour and bake in the oven for 35–45 minutes until the bottom of the tin sounds hollow when you tap it. Turn out onto a wire rack to cool.

CRISPY SUPER CRACKERS

These crackers are simple to make and store well for when you need a quick snack or light lunch on the run. Other superseeds to experiment with include poppy and chia seeds.

Makes about 30 crackers

450 g/1 lb/3½ cups wholemeal (whole-wheat) spelt flour

1 tsp unrefined salt

50 g/2 oz/⅓ cup sesame seeds

50 g/2 oz/⅓ cup flaxseeds

50 g/2 oz/⅓ cup pumpkin seeds, ground

250 ml/8 fl oz/1 cup water

1 tbsp runny honey or maple syrup

4 tbsp extra virgin olive oil, plus extra for greasing

50 g/2 oz/⅓ cup mixed sesame, sunflower and pumpkin seeds, for topping

1 tbsp unsweetened hemp milk

Combine the flour, salt, sesame seeds, flaxseeds and ground pumpkin seeds together in a bowl. In a separate bowl, whisk the water, honey or maple syrup and olive oil together.

Mix the dry and wet ingredients together to form a stiff dough. On an oiled surface, knead the dough for 5 minutes, then return to the bowl and leave to stand for 20 minutes.

Preheat the oven to 180°C/375°F/Gas Mark 4. Line 2–3 baking trays (pans) with baking parchment.

On the oiled work surface, roll the dough out to a thickness of 3 mm/⅛ inch (do this in batches if you have restricted space). Using a ruler and a sharp knife or pizza cutter, cut the dough into rectangles, about 5 x 10 cm/2 x 4 inches each.

Mix the topping seeds with the hemp milk and scatter the seed mix over the crackers. Place the seeded crackers onto the prepared trays, close together but not touching. Bake the crackers for 15–18 minutes until lightly browned. Turn the oven off, open the door for 30 seconds to release the steam, and close again. Leave the trays in the residual heat of the oven for 10–15 minutes for extra crispness*. Transfer to a wire rack to cool.

Note:

If they don't crisp up once they are cool, put them back in a preheated oven for a further 5–7 minutes.

MULTI-SEED OAT LOAF

This is a lovely rustic loaf that is filling and healthy – it is packed with superfood goodness. Try it toasted for breakfast, with reduced-sugar jam or slices of avocado and tomato sprinkled with salt and freshly ground black pepper.

Makes 1 loaf

coconut oil, for greasing

100 g/3½ oz/⅔ cup rolled oats

300 g/11 oz/2⅓ cups white spelt flour, plus extra for dusting

50 g/2 oz/⅓ cup sunflower seeds, coarsely ground

50 g/2 oz/⅓ cup flaxseeds, coarsely ground

2½ tsp easy-blend dried yeast (active dry yeast)

1 tsp unrefined salt

5 tbsp olive oil

250 ml/8 fl oz/1 cup unsweetened oat milk, plus extra for glazing

1 tbsp honey or maple syrup

jumbo oats, flaxseeds and sunflower seeds, for topping

Grease a 900 g/2 lb loaf tin (pan) with coconut oil.

In a blender jug or spice grinder, blitz the rolled oats into a flour.

In a large mixing bowl, combine the flours, ground sunflower seeds, ground flaxseeds, yeast and salt.

Whisk the olive oil, oat milk and honey or maple syrup together in a jug. Stir the wet ingredients into the dry ingredients and mix thoroughly. Knead the dough on a floured work surface for 5–10 minutes until it feels smooth and pliable.

Put the dough back into the bowl, cover and leave to rise in a warm place until doubled in size, about 50–60 minutes. When the dough has doubled in size, knead again for several minutes*.

Shape the dough, brush the top with oat milk and sprinkle over jumbo oats, flaxseeds and sunflower seeds. Place in the loaf tin and cover with a cloth. Leave to rise in a warm place for 60 minutes.

Preheat the oven to 180°C/350°F/Gas Mark 4.

Bake in the oven for 35–40 minutes until the bottom of the tin sounds hollow when tapped. Turn out onto a wire rack and leave to cool.

Note:

For a fast loaf, skip this step and leave to rise only once in the tin, sprinkled with the oats and seeds, covered with a cloth.

BEETROOT TART
with Horseradish

The contrast of the earthy sweetness of the beetroot (beet) and the sharp freshness of the horseradish make this tart a sophisticated delight. It looks wonderful paired with the bright leaves of a green salad.

Serves

olive oil or butter, for greasing

225 g/8 oz ready-made shortcrust pastry or oat-crust (*see* page 181)

3 tbsp plain (all-purpose) flour, plus extra for dusting

2 tbsp extra virgin olive oil

1 small red onion, peeled and roughly diced

1 garlic clove, peeled and very finely chopped

400 g/14 oz cooked peeled beetroot (beet)

½ tsp unrefined salt

freshly ground black pepper

1 tbsp grated fresh horseradish (or 1 tsp bought horseradish sauce)

2 heaped tsp homemade or bought horseradish sauce

For the horseradish sauce (optional)

3 tbsp finely grated fresh horseradish root, soaked in 2 tbsp hot water

1 tbsp white wine vinegar

½ tsp English mustard

½ tsp honey

3 tbsp double cream or oat cream

salt and freshly ground black pepper

Preheat the oven to 180°C/350°F/Gas Mark 4. Grease an 18 cm/7 inch fluted pie tin (pan) with olive oil or butter.

To make the homemade horseradish sauce, if using, drain the grated horseradish root and mix together with the rest of the sauce ingredients. Set aside.

For the tart, roll the pastry into a round on a floured work surface and lay it in the pie tin, gently pressing into the bottom and sides, then cut off any surplus pastry. (If using the oat crust dough don't roll it, just press the pastry into the tin with wet fingertips.) Prick the base all over with a fork and bake for 7 minutes. Remove from the oven, gently pushing the base flat if necessary. Set side.

Heat the olive oil in small pan over a medium-low heat and sauté the onion until translucent. Add the garlic and cook for another minute.

Blend the cooked onion and garlic with the beetroot (beet), salt and pepper until smooth. Thoroughly stir in the 1 tablespoon grated horseradish (or 1 teaspoon bought horseradish sauce).

Fill the pastry shell with the beetroot mixture. Gently swirl through the 2 heaped teaspoons homemade (or bought) horseradish sauce, then bake in the oven for 30 minutes.

Serve warm with a green salad.

SWEET TREATS

SORGHUM-CRUST PECAN PIE

This vegan, gluten-free and refined-sugar-free pecan pie is deliciously decadent. Serve it with chilled coconut cream for dessert or as it is for a luxurious afternoon tea.

Serves 8 - 10

For the crust

75 g/3 oz/⅓ cup cold coconut oil,
   plus extra for greasing
150 g/5 oz/1⅓ cups sorghum flour
pinch unrefined salt
2 tsp xanthan gum
2 tsp date syrup
2–4 tbsp water

For the filling

150 g/5 oz/1⅓ cups chopped pecans
175 ml/6 fl oz/scant ¾ cup date syrup
75 ml/3 fl oz/¼ cup + 1 tbsp water
1–2 tbsp bourbon or 1 tbsp water
2 tbsp nut butter of your choice, such as almond butter
40 g/1½ oz/⅓ cup ground flaxseed (flax meal)
1½ tsp sugar-free vanilla extract
½ tsp salt
pecans, to decorate

Preheat the oven to 180°C/350°F/Gas Mark 4. Grease a 22 cm/9 inch loose-bottomed pie tin (pan) with coconut oil.

For the pastry, mix the flour, salt and xanthan gum in a mixing bowl. Rub in the cold coconut oil and date syrup with your fingertips until the mixture resembles fine breadcrumbs. Rub in the enough of the water for the pastry to come together. Press into the pie tin. Prick the bottom all over with a fork and bake for 7 minutes. Remove from the oven.

Stir all the filling ingredients, except the pecans for decorating, together in a bowl. Chill for 20 minutes so that the ground flaxseed (flax meal) swells and thickens the mixture. Spoon the thickened filling into the crust. Decorate the top with pecans and bake in the oven for 35 minutes. Turn off the oven, leaving the pie to rest inside with the door closed for a further 10 minutes. Remove from the oven and allow to cool in the tin.

RAW BRAZIL BALLS

These Brazil balls are super quick and easy to make as they don't require cooking. They make a great mid-morning pick-me-up as well as being a super-healthy after-school snack for kids.

Makes about 10

50 g/2 oz/⅓ cup rolled oats

2 tbsp melted coconut oil

3 tbsp almond butter

½ tsp sugar-free vanilla extract

pinch unrefined salt

1 tbsp honey or maple syrup

100 g/3½ oz/¾ cup Brazil nuts, chopped into small pieces

25 g/1 oz/¼ cup raisins

In a blender jug or spice grinder, blitz the rolled oats into a flour.

In a slightly warmed mixing bowl, stir the melted coconut oil, almond butter, vanilla, salt and honey or maple syrup together. Add the Brazil nuts, raisins and oat flour and mix thoroughly.

Using the palms of your hands, roll about 1 tablespoon of the mixture into a ball. Continue like this until the mixture is used up. Put the balls in the refrigerator to set.

Store in a sealed container in the refrigerator for up to 3 weeks, or freeze for up to 6 weeks.

MATCHA CURD TARTLETS

These little beauties are a gorgeous dinner party dessert or special occasion treat. I save time by making them with a locally made additive-free lemon curd, but you can always make your own if you enjoy making preserves.

Makes 4

For the crust

250 g/9 oz gluten-free digestive (Graham crackers without chocolate coating) or shortbread biscuits (cookies)
100 g/3½ oz/7 tbsp butter

For the filling

250 g/9 oz good-quality lemon curd
1 tsp matcha powder, sifted, plus extra for dusting

Line four 8 cm/3 inch loose-bottomed fluted tartlet tins (pans) with plastic wrap.

Put the biscuits (crackers or cookies) into a clean plastic bag and bash with a rolling pin until they become fine crumbs. Add the crumbs to a bowl and stir in the melted butter. Divide the mixture between the tartlet tins and press evenly over the bottom and sides to create the tartlet shells. Chill in the refrigerator for 30 minutes.

Thoroughly combine the lemon curd with the sifted matcha powder and divide evenly between each tartlet. Smooth the top with a spoon and put back in the refrigerator to chill for 1–2 hours.

To serve, carefully remove each tartlet from its tin and plastic wrap and top with a fine dusting of matcha powder.

CHIA PUDDING WITH BERRIES

Chia seeds are incredibly versatile and fun to cook with. Their naturally glutinous quality is great for creating a layered 'jelly' dessert that is super healthy and fresh. Mix it up a bit and experiment with your favourite fruit combinations.

Makes 2

For the fruit jelly layer

125 g/4 oz/1 cup raspberries

2 tsp chia seeds

2 tsp honey or date syrup

For the milk jelly layer

150 ml/¼ pint/⅔ cup unsweetened hemp milk

150 ml/¼ pint/⅔ cup dairy-free cream,
   such as oat cream

1½ tbsp honey or maple syrup

½ tsp sugar-free vanilla extract

3 tbsp chia seeds

For the topping

mixed fresh berries, such
   as raspberries and
   blackberries

walnuts

Using a blender, purée all the fruit jelly ingredients until smooth. Spoon into the bottom of two glasses and smooth the top. Place in the refrigerator to set.

In a small mixing bowl, combine all the milk jelly layer ingredients. Leave to stand for 20–30 minutes, stirring regularly, until the mixture thickens and the chia seeds are evenly distributed. Pour on top of the fruit jelly layer and smooth the top. Chill in the refrigerator for at least 1 hour until set.

Just before serving, top with fresh berries and walnuts.

COCONUT PANCAKES

Traditional pancakes are not usually on the list of healthy things to eat. These coconut pancakes are gluten-free and dairy-free, with no refined sugar – as guilt-free as you can get! For extra pizzazz, add the zest of an orange to the vanilla syrup.

Makes 15–20 pancakes

For the vanilla syrup

5 tbsp maple syrup

½ tsp sugar-free vanilla extract

For the pancakes

4 medium organic eggs

250 ml/8 fl oz/1 cup unsweetened coconut milk

2 tsp sugar-free vanilla extract

¼ tsp sea salt

1 tbsp honey or maple syrup

65 g/2½ oz/⅔ cup coconut flour

1 tsp bicarbonate of soda (baking soda)

coconut oil, for frying

chopped almonds, for sprinkling

Make the vanilla syrup by warming the maple syrup and vanilla together in a small pan over a low heat. Set aside.

To make the pancakes, blend all the pancake ingredients, except the coconut oil and chopped almonds, until smooth.

In a frying pan, melt the coconut oil over a medium-high heat. Cook the pancakes in batches: when the oil is hot, spoon in 2 tablespoons of mixture per pancake and allow to spread naturally into a round. Cook for 3–4 minutes until bubbles form on the top and the bottom is golden. Flip the pancakes and cook for a further 2 minutes so that both sides are golden. Keep warm while you cook the remaining pancakes.

When all the pancakes are cooked, stack them on a warmed plate. Drizzle with the vanilla syrup and sprinkle with chopped almonds before serving.

BLUEBERRY CHEESECAKE

This special occasion cake is a no-bake raw and vegan 'cheesecake'. For a super-smooth base and filling, soak the dates and cashews overnight before making the recipe. The topping is optional, but it makes it that extra bit special.

Makes 12 slices

For the base

10 pitted Medjool dates

100 g/3½ oz/1 cup walnuts

pinch unrefined salt

½ tsp sugar-free vanilla extract

3 tbsp melted coconut oil

2 tbsp cocoa powder

For the topping (optional)

125 g/4 oz/1 cup blueberries

coconut flakes

edible flowers

For the filling

225 g/8 oz/2 cups cashews

1 tbsp lemon zest (about 1½ lemons)

4 tbsp lemon juice

6 tbsp melted coconut oil

4 tbsp water

2 tbsp sugar-free vanilla extract

½ tsp nutritional yeast

200 g/7 oz/1⅔ cups blueberries

Line an 18 cm/7 inch loose-bottomed cake tin (pan) with plastic wrap.

For the base, soak the pitted dates in hot water until softened, about 30–60 minutes or overnight. Grind the walnuts in a spice grinder or mini food processor.

Using a blender, purée the softened dates with the salt, vanilla and melted coconut oil. In a bowl, stir together the date purée, the ground walnuts and cocoa powder. Spoon into the cake tin and smooth the top with the back of a spoon. Freeze while you make the filling.

Blend all the filling ingredients, except the blueberries, until completely smooth. Add the blueberries and blend again until most but not all the blueberries have been blended in. Remove the cake tin from the freezer and spoon the filling on top of the base, smoothing with the back of a spoon. Return to the freezer or refrigerator for 1–4 hours until set firm.

To decorate, scatter over the blueberries, coconut flakes and edible flowers, if using.

SPICED GOJI BROWNIES

These dark chocolate brownies are subtly spicy. They are packed full of superfood loveliness to give you energy when you need it. You can eat them fresh or freeze for another time, so they are great for surprise visitors.

Makes 8 brownies

50 g/2 oz/⅓ cup dried dates

150 ml/¼ pint/⅔ cup just-boiled water

100 g/3½ oz/1 cup ground almonds

50 g/2 oz/½ cup sifted cocoa powder

1 tbsp ground cinnamon

2 tsp ground ginger

pinch unrefined salt

5 tbsp melted coconut oil

1 tsp sugar-free vanilla extract

2–3 tbsp honey or maple syrup

50 g/2 oz/½ cup shelled pistachios

50 g/2 oz/½ cup goji berries

50 g/2 oz/⅓ cup toasted sunflower seeds

100 g/3½ oz bar dark chocolate, broken into pieces

Soak the dates in the just-boiled water for at least 1 hour. Line a 15 x 22 cm/6 x 9 inch baking dish with plastic wrap.

In a food processor or mixing bowl, thoroughly mix the ground almonds, cocoa powder, ground cinnamon, ground ginger and salt together.

Using a blender, blitz the dates, date soaking water, melted coconut oil, vanilla and 2 tablespoons of honey or maple syrup until smooth. Stir the wet ingredients into the dry ingredients. Next, stir in the pistachios, goji berries and sunflower seeds. Taste and add another tablespoon of honey or maple syrup if you prefer your brownies sweeter. Spoon the mixture into the baking dish and smooth over with a wet spatula.

Gently melt the chocolate in a heatproof bowl set over a pan of boiling water. Don't let the base of the bowl touch the water. Using a spoon, drizzle the melted chocolate over the brownie mix and chill in the refrigerator until set.

Once set, remove from the dish and plastic wrap. Cut into 8 brownies with a sharp knife. Store in a sealed container in the refrigerator for up to 1 week, or freeze individually for up to 1 month.

MATCHA ICE CREAM

I simply love the colour of this superfood dairy-free ice-cream. For double deliciousness, serve it with the matcha curd tartlets on page 204, or with chopped kiwi fruits and fresh raspberries topped with a drizzle of oat cream.

Serves 4

250 ml/8 fl oz/1 cup unsweetened almond milk
125 g/4 oz/⅓ cup honey
2 egg yolks
150 ml/¼ pint/⅔ cup oat cream
1 tsp matcha powder

Warm the almond milk and honey in a pan over a medium heat until just below boiling point, stirring until the honey is melted and well mixed in.

Whisk the egg yolks in a mixing bowl, then whisk in the oat cream and matcha powder. Pour in the hot milk and honey and whisk again. Using a sieve (strainer), strain the mixture into a clean bowl. Leave until cold.

Once cold, pour the mixture into an ice-cream maker, churning following the manufacturer's instructions. If you do not have an ice-cream maker, put the ice-cream mixture into a freezerproof bowl in the freezer and whisk every 15 minutes or so until frozen (usually about 2–3 hours).

Before eating, put the ice cream in the refrigerator for 20 minutes to soften a little.

MACA COCONUT ENERGY BALLS

These energy balls are great for when you need a mid-morning or mid-afternoon boost. Make up a big batch and freeze them, so that you never run out of healthy treats to keep you away from the biscuits (cookies) and sweets (candies).

Makes 10–12

100 g/3½ oz/¾ cup rolled oats

100 g/3½ oz/1 cup ground almonds

4 tbsp coconut oil

zest of 1 orange

1 tbsp maca powder

1 tsp ground turmeric

1 tsp sugar-free vanilla extract

3 tbsp honey or maple syrup

desiccated (unsweetened shredded dry) coconut, for rolling

In a blender jug or spice grinder, blitz the rolled oats into a flour.

Combine all the ingredients, except the desiccated (unsweetened shredded dry) coconut for rolling, in a bowl. One tablespoon at a time, roll the mixture into balls between the palms of your hands, wetting your hands to stop the mixture sticking, if necessary.

Pour the desiccated coconut onto a side plate and roll each ball in the coconut. Once all the balls are coated, put them in the refrigerator to set.

Store in a sealed container in the refrigerator for up to 1 week, or freeze for up to 1 month.

NUTTY LUCUMA BARS

I love the flavour of toasted nuts. Here, it combines beautifully with the caramel taste of the lucuma and the tartness of the cranberries to give you a sophisticated healthy treat.

Makes 9 bars

150 g/5 oz/1 cup mixed nuts, such as Brazils, hazelnuts/filberts, almonds

200 g/7 oz/1⅓ cups rolled oats

4 tbsp lucuma powder

1 large pinch unrefined salt

50 g/2 oz/½ cup dried cranberries (no added sugar), chopped

2 tbsp melted coconut oil

1 tsp sugar-free vanilla extract

2 tbsp honey or maple syrup

Line a 15 x 15 cm/6 x 6 inch high-sided baking tray (baking pan) with plastic wrap.

Lay the nuts out in a single layer on another baking tray and roast in the oven for 10–15 minutes, stirring halfway through. Remove from the oven and leave to cool. Once cool, grind in a spice grinder or blender.

Blitz the rolled oats into a fine flour in a jug blender or spice grinder.

Thoroughly combine the ground nuts, oat flour, lucuma powder, salt, chopped cranberries, melted coconut oil, vanilla and honey or maple syrup in a mixing bowl. Press the mixture into the baking tray and set in the refrigerator.

Remove from the baking tray and cut into bars. Store in a sealed container in the refrigerator for up to 1 month, or freeze for up to 6 weeks.

INDEX

Entries with upper-case initials indicate recipes.

If you enjoyed this book please sign up for updates,
information and offers on further titles in this series at
www.flametreepublishing.com